CW00348192

FlatSpin

A Comedy

Alan Ayckbourn

A SAMUEL FRENCH ACTING EDITION

FOUNDED 1830

SAMUELFRENCH-LONDON.CO.UK
SAMUELFRENCH.COM

ISBN 978-0-573-11565-3

www.samuelfrench-london.co.uk

www.samuelfrench.com

FOR AMATEUR PRODUCTION ENQUIRIES

UNITED KINGDOM AND WORLD
EXCLUDING NORTH AMERICA
plays@SamuelFrench-London.co.uk
020 7255 4302/01

Each title is subject to availability from Samuel French,

depending upon country of performance.

FLATSPIN

First performed at the Stephen Joseph Theatre, Scarborough, on 3rd July 2001. The same production was subsequently presented by Michael Codron, Lee Dean, Michael Linnit, David Ian for ClearChannel Entertainment and Andrew Lloyd Webber, at the Duchess Theatre, London, on 7th September 2002. The cast was as follows:

Annette Sefton-Wilcox	Beth Tuckey
Rosie Seymore	Alison Pargeter
Sam Berryman	Bill Champion
Edna Stricken	Jacqueline King
Maurice Whickett	Robert Austin
Tracy Taylor	Saskia Butler
Tommy Angel	Tim Faraday

Directed by Alan Ayckbourn
Designed by Roger Glossop
Lighting design by Mick Hughes
Costume design by Christine Wall

CHARACTERS

Annette Sefton-Wilcox, 30s
Rosie Seymore, 20s
Sam Berryman, 30s
Edna Stricken, 40s
Maurice Whickett, 50s
Tracy Taylor, 20s
Tommy Angel, 30s

The action of the play takes place in a riverside apartment
in London's Docklands

ACT I
Scene 1 August Bank Holiday Monday, noon
Scene 2 The same day 6.30 p.m.

ACT II
Scene 1 A few minutes later
Scene 2 Thirty minutes later

Time—the present

Plays by Alan Ayckbourn published by Samuel French Ltd

Absent Friends
Absurd Person Singular
Bedroom Farce
Body Language
Callisto 5
The Champion of Paribanou
A Chorus of Disapproval
Communicating Doors
Confusions
A Cut in the Rates
Dreams from a Summer House (with John Pattison)
Ernie's Incredible Illucinations
Family Circles
Gizmo
Henceforward...
House & Garden
How the Other Half Loves
Intimate Exchanges (Volume 1 and Volume 2)
It Could Be Any One of Us
Joking Apart
Just Between Ourselves
Living Together
Man of the Moment
Mixed Doubles (*with other authors*)
Mr A's Amazing Maze Plays
Mr Whatnot
My Very Own Story
The Norman Conquests
Relatively Speaking
The Revengers' Comedies
Round and Round the Garden
Season's Greetings
Sisterly Feelings
A Small Family Business
Snake in the Grass
Suburban Strains (with Paul Todd)
Table Manners
Taking Steps
Ten Times Table
Things We Do For Love
This is Where We Came In
Time and Time Again
Time of My Life
Tons of Money (*revisor*)
Way Upstream
Wildest Dreams
Wolf at the Door (*adapter*)
Woman in Mind
A Word from Our Sponsor (with John Pattison)

ACT I

SCENE 1

A riverside apartment on the Thames, somewhere in London's Docklands. August Bank Holiday Monday. Noon

It's a corporately owned flat, impersonal, with little clue or indeed sign of the inhabitant. A main sitting area and an adjoining walk-through kitchen/ dining area. Sliding windows at one end of the sitting area lead on to a small riverside balcony. At the other end of this sitting area, a well-stocked bar. Near the window, a desk and chair. On the desk, a discreetly placed book. A sofa, an armchair and a heavy coffee table. A few quite healthy pot plants dotted around. Leading off this area is a short hallway which leads directly to the front door. Also two archways leading to another area visible to us, the common kitchen/dining space. The kitchen end is well equipped, evidently regularly cleaned, but has clearly not been used for some time. It has an almost spartan tidiness. The other end has a small dining table with four chairs. Leading from this in turn is a further door to the offstage bedroom

It is around noon in the midst of an August Bank Holiday heatwave. Bright sunshine floods the room

After a second, Annette, the managing agents' representative, enters. She is in her late thirties, smartly dressed in a business suit. She carries a large set of master keys. With her is Rosie, mid-twenties, casually dressed. She carries a notebook and pencil in which she occasionally makes an addition or checks an entry

Annette (*swiftly, in full flow, as they enter*) ...and this one you'll have very little bother with at all. Number 3C, Mrs Rupelford. R—U—P... Got her on your list, have you?

Rosie (*consulting her notes*) Yes, yes, Rupelford. Water plants ... flush toilets regularly ... check round generally...

Annette Spot on. There's a cleaner comes in every month and gives it a good going over, which is all it basically needs, of course, because this woman never sets foot in the place.

Rosie Never?

Annette Not so far as anyone can gather. Let's say that no-one's ever seen her. Still, it doesn't bother us, it's a corporate let, they pay the rent—if they want to waste their money it's up to them, isn't it? No, to be perfectly fair, I think Joanna Rupelford's job does entail an awful lot of overseas travel, so far as I can gather—between the two of us, I think she's oil, actually—all the same, you'd think for the amount of time she was in London it would be cheaper to stick the woman in a hotel, wouldn't it? Still, as I say, who are we...? Now, all perfectly clear so far, is it?

Rosie Yes, I think so, Mrs Sefton-Wilcox.

Annette Annette, please.

Rosie Annette, sorry. (*She consults her notes*) 7B—Mrs Truffick. Water plants weekly, air flat occasionally when away. General check round.

Annette Yes, Ann Truffick's a sheer delight. You'll have absolutely no trouble with her.

Rosie 5D—Mr and Mrs Warmlow. Check intermittent shower drip—occasional weekend feed fish.

Annette Yes, and whatever else, don't forget to do that. They're the most terrible fusspots, both of them. If their blessed fish starve to death, we'll never hear the end of it. Bane of all our lives, I can tell you, the Warmlows. You won't believe it but they're actually in the midst of litigation with the window cleaner.

Rosie Really?

Annette They're retired, of course, so they've nothing else to do but write us complaining letters...

Rosie (*sympathetically*) Yes, well...

Annette Why they can't behave like normal retired people, buy somewhere abroad and die of drink gracefully, I can't imagine. Sorry, do carry on, Rose. Rose, isn't it?

Rosie Rosie.

Annette Rosie, of course. How pretty.

Rosie Thank you. Er—4A—Mr Cheetham. Water plants when advised. Feed budgie on Thursdays.

Annette Yes, now as I say, Mr Cheetham is the weeniest bit odd. The plants are all plastic and the bird cage is empty, but go through the motions. He's perfectly harmless. Secretly, I think he's just desperate for company.

Rosie Right. 3C—Mrs Rupelford—water plants—flush toilets—general check round.

Annette Oh, spot on, well done. I'll say again, we're all so, so grateful to you for stepping in like this, Rosie. I mean, normally, if one of our janitors is away for more than a day, we arrange proper cover, naturally we do. But of course, with your uncle and aunt due back today, we never——

Rosie No, it was all very sudden...

Annette Such unfortunate timing. Are they both all right, by the way?

Rosie Yes, just a little shaken. I spoke to them earlier. They're just keeping them in overnight for observation. Whiplash.

Annette The traffic gets worse and worse, doesn't it? I mean, normally Milton—Mr Granger—would be here to cover for your uncle. But he went off late last night to Benidorm. And on top of everything else it's this wretched Bank Holiday. There's one every other week these days, isn't there? Not that it makes a blind bit of difference to me—I just soldier on regardless—(*she laughs*)—must be in the wrong job, mustn't I?—anyway, as I say, we're all frightfully grateful to you, Rosie. What a stroke of luck you were free!

Rosie Yes, well, it happens I wasn't working this weekend so...

Annette Yes, now what is it you do again? Your uncle did tell me once, I think—are you still a student?

Rosie No, I'm an actor.

Annette An actress! Oh, how super. Ought I to know you?

Rosie No, I shouldn't think so...

Annette I mean, have you been in anything I'd have seen on the box—not that I ever actually have time to watch it, of course. I mean, the number of occasions I actually manage to sit down and see a whole programme...

Rosie Well, it wouldn't really matter if you had because I haven't really been in anything...

Annette No, no, no, that's not true. Come to think of it, you do seem familiar now I look at you. I have seen you in something, I'm sure...

Rosie I think it's unlikely. Unless you've been to Crewkerne lately.

Annette Crewkerne? Is that a series?

Rosie No, it's a place. I was touring with a children's company that's based there.

Annette Where on earth is Crewkerne?

Rosie Somerset.

Annette Heavens. Yonks away.

Rosie Certainly is.

Annette What made you choose there? I didn't even know they did television in Somerset.

Rosie No, this was theatre.

Annette Theatre. Oh. You're a theatre actress, then?

Rosie No. Any sort. I'm not really fussy.

Annette So, do you come from Somerset?

Rosie No. Nottingham, actually.

Annette So what made you choose Crewkerne?

Rosie Well, fancied the challenge. You know.

Annette Wonderful. What fun. It must have been enormous fun, wasn't it?

Rosie Yes. Eight weeks touring. Ten a.m. shows in a van. Fitting up at nine a.m. in school halls. Changing in the lavatories.

Annette Golly. What were you playing?

Rosie *The Princess and the Pea.*

Annette Oh, I say! Which one were you? (*She laughs a lot*)
Rosie (*smiling thinly*) Neither.
Annette Sorry, I was only joking. Which part did you take, then?
Rosie Actually. I played a rabbit.
Annette A rabbit? Heavens!
Rosie Yes.
Annette Golly. That's dedication. All the way to Crewkerne to be a rabbit.
Rosie (*getting sick of this*) Well. There you go.
Annette Still, I suppose that's how Meryl Streep must have started, mustn't she?
Rosie I doubt it somehow.
Annette Tell me, are you a—what do you call it?—a method actress? Did you prepare by crouching in fields and eating lettuce and things? I was reading somewhere that Robert De Niro always does that sort of thing...
Rosie Does he? No, I honestly just put on the ears, did the job and took the money, actually. Such as it was...
Annette Ears! Yes, of course. You must have had ears! How sweet! Did you have a little white tail as well?
Rosie Yes. The works. Listen, Annette, was there anything else or should I—?
Annette Yes, I'd imagine you'd make a lovely rabbit. You're quite petite, aren't you? That would help, being very small.
Rosie Fairly small, yes.
Annette I say, I do hope this job isn't going to be too much for you...
Rosie No, well, if necessary I'll have to climb on a box, won't I?
Annette No, seriously, I meant there's some quite hefty bin work, you know. A lot of heavy mopping.
Rosie Well, I'll probably manage to lift the mop OK. Don't worry.
Annette No, what I meant was...
Rosie I work out quite regularly.
Annette Yes, I suppose you'd need to. Tell me, when you play rabbits, do you need to do special—?
Rosie Look, I don't think I'm going to be playing many more rabbits, actually.
Annette No?
Rosie No. I think I've probably given my rabbit. I'm planning to move on.
Annette What next? A horse? (*She laughs*)

Rosie stares at her. She's had it up to here with this woman

Only joking. Sorry.
Rosie (*rather tense*) Actually, if everything goes according to plan, I think I'm about to play a major lead in a classic television serial on BBC One.

Annette Oh. Spot on! Of course, I don't really watch those classic things because I can never guarantee to see the next episode, the life I lead.

Rosie Well, never mind. I expect a lot of people will.

Annette No doubt. Most of them seem to have time to waste these days, don't they? So when are you on? I'll try and catch you.

Rosie Well, it hasn't started yet. I mean, I'm still waiting for final confirmation that I've got it but my agent says it's ninety per cent certain.

Annette Jolly good. No more rabbits then?

Rosie 'Fraid not.

Annette Unless you're doing *Watership Down*, of course. (*She laughs merrily*)

Rosie stares at her, icily

Sorry. Only joking. Well, I can't stand around. I must get on.

Rosie You must.

Annette Now, you're absolutely clear on everything, are you?

Rosie Yes.

Annette You've got my card anyway, haven't you? In case of a real emergency. Otherwise, Milton—Mr Granger—will be here first thing Wednesday morning to take over. All right?

Rosie Thank you.

Annette No, thank *you*, Rosie. Really. Sincerely. Well, I suppose I must brave the heat again. It's unbearable today, isn't it? Like an oven out there. Must be in the nineties. There's something terribly wrong with the climate lately, if you ask me. Tell you what, you might as well get started in here whilst you're at it, mightn't you? Water Joanna Rupelford's plants. They look as if they're wilting.

Rosie I'll do that.

Annette Try not to nibble them, though, won't you? (*She peals with laughter*) Sorry. Only joking. Byeee!

Annette goes out of the front door, still laughing

Rosie pulls a face

Rosie (*faintly reminiscent of Annette's voice*) Spot on! (*She unlocks and slides open the windows*)

The sounds of the river fill the room. Rosie steps out cautiously and grips the balcony rail

(*Leaning out and looking to her right*) Fantastical! Spot on! (*She comes in*

again, leaving the windows open) Right, little plants. Let me deal with you.
(She feels the base of one of them. Sympathetically) Oh. Thirsty, little one.
Thirsty. One moment. *(She consults her list)* 3C. Watering can under sink.
Under sink. Sink. The sink, I sink, is in here! *(She goes to the sink and,
opening the cupboard beneath it, finds a small domestic watering can)*
Aha! *(Annette's voice again)* Spot on. Spot on. *(She fills the watering can
and starts watering the plants. She stops by the desk, is about to water the
plant and then, out of curiosity, picks up the solitary book lying there. She
reads)* Swinburne, *Collected Poems*. Heavens! *(She reads the inside
cover)* This book belongs to Joanna Rupelford. *(She tries out the name a
little)* Joanna Rupelford! Joanna Rupelford! *(She starts to water the plant)*
And tonight's very special guest—ladies and gentlemen—Joanna
Rupelford! *(She makes applause noises with her mouth)*

In her bag, her mobile phone rings

Oh, God! This is it! This must be it! *(She dives for her phone and retrieves
it. She studies the screen, disappointed)* Oh. *(She answers)* Hi, Cat. No, not
yet... I thought you were Jason... No, he hasn't ... well, he said some time
this morning ... but then they said that yesterday... Oh, who cares? ... If
I get it, I get it, love. If I don't, too bad... *(She returns to the plant as she
speaks and finishes watering it)* Well, it's the only way, isn't it? ... Yes,
I'll talk to you later, sweet. Better leave the line clear. Yep. OK. 'Bye, Cat.
*(She disconnects and puts the phone on the desk and moves to the next
plant. Quietly and with deep conviction)* I would like to thank everyone
concerned. An award is never truly won by a single individual. In the end,
it's all about teamwork. *(She moves to the third plant)* And, ladies and
gentlemen, let's face it, the fact that you have voted me best actress of all
time in the entire universe ever is neither here nor there. All I would like
to say——

*On the desk, her mobile rings again. She puts down the watering can
hurriedly, rushes back to the desk and, glancing at the screen, prepares to
answer it*

Oh, God! Please God! *(She takes a deep breath and answers. Exaggeratedly
calm)* Hi, Jason! Good morning. Yes? ... Yes? ... Oh that, yes...
Practically forgotten about that, so long ago... Uh-huh. ... Yep. ... Well,
that's nice of them... Yes, that's really nice they said that ... yep... I think
I did, yes... Yes, but do they want me, Jason? ... *(She listens)* Yes, but do
they? ... Jason, do they want *me*? ... Do they want me or her? ... Yep. Yep.
OK. No, that's fine... No, I'm not. Not at all. No. Yes, well ... maybe they
will ... yep. OK. Yes, no, I'm quite busy just now ... thanks all the same.

Another time. Yes, thank you. I will. Don't worry. 'Bye. (*She stands very dejected, on the verge of tears*) Oh. (*She punches out a number*) Hi, Cat. It's me again. Yes, I just heard. No, in the end they went for her. I thought they would, I really did. No, well, obviously they felt I was... No. I'm fine about it. Really. Just fine. No, I feel absolutely... (*Suddenly the tears are ebbing up*) It's just—God, Cat—I could have at least got a job, couldn't I? I deserve that surely? I've given up smoking, I've got no money and since Davie walked out, I haven't even had decent sex for six months, I mean I deserve something, don't I? It's just not fair, it really isn't——

The doorbell rings

Oh, God! Someone's at the door, I'll call you back, Cat. Yes.

The doorbell rings again. She disconnects

It'll be that bloody Annette Sefton-Wilcox again, I know it. (*She gets up and goes to the kitchen where she grabs some kitchen roll and attempts to tidy herself up. She goes and opens the front door*)

Sam, in his thirties, stands there

Sam (*smiling*) Hi!
Rosie (*despite her current state, impressed*) Oh.
Sam Sorry. Am I...
Rosie What?
Sam Am I—interrupting something?
Rosie No, no.
Sam Sam. Hallo.
Rosie Oh, yes?
Sam Sam Berryman. Flat 3B. From next door.
Rosie Oh.
Sam I know we haven't met. I've been your neighbour for six months.
Rosie Oh, no. I'm not——
Sam I heard your front door close. I knew you must be back. (*He moves past her*) What a lovely flat. Do you mind?
Rosie (*feebly*) Listen...
Sam (*moving towards the open window*) Oh, look at this. You have the view. You definitely have the view, don't you?
Rosie No, I should explain, I'm not——
Sam I'm at the back there so all I have is the park. I mean, the park's nice enough. But the river is better. (*He steps outside on to the balcony*) God! Look at this. Isn't this wonderful!

Rosie (*following him out there*) Listen, before you go on, I really must...
Sam (*craning out to his right*) Is that Tower Bridge? Yes, Tower Bridge!
Rosie ...can I just say—?
Sam (*leaning out the other way*) Look, you can even see the Dome, can't you? This is just amazing. You're so lucky!
Rosie (*forcefully*) Would you please listen to me a minute! Please.
Sam Sorry?
Rosie I'm afraid you've got it all wrong...
Sam That's not the Dome?
Rosie No! Of course it's the Dome. Don't be so stupid. All I'm saying is, I'm— (*She stops. She's not yet fully recovered*) Sorry.
Sam You all right?
Rosie Of course I'm all right.
Sam Have you been crying?
Rosie Of course I haven't. It's nothing at all. It's just I had a—(*unable to contain herself any longer*)—a bit of bad news—— (*She totters*)
Sam (*catching her arm*) Hey! Hey! Hey! Come on! Sit down. Come on, sit down!

He steers Rosie, now weeping openly, back into the room and sits her down

You say you've had bad news—?
Rosie Yes.
Sam Do you want to talk about it? What's happened? Have you recently lost someone?
Rosie Just now... They just told me...
Sam Oh, dear God...
Rosie ...he just phoned me...
Sam ...that's terrible.
Rosie I would have been perfect for her. I know I would...
Sam Her? This was someone very close to you, was it?
Rosie I was as close as that. It was between me and this other girl...
Sam (*understanding at last*) I see, I see. Hell, I'm sorry. Believe me, you're not unique. It happens to all of us, sooner or later.
Rosie (*recovering slightly*) Does it?
Sam (*smiling*) Believe it or not—even to me.
Rosie Are you an actor, then?
Sam A what?
Rosie An actor?
Sam No.
Rosie (*rather mystified*) Oh.
Sam I'm an investment consultant.
Rosie Ah.

Sam Can I get you something? A cup of tea? A brandy?

Rosie (*indicating her running nose*) Do you have a—? I just need a...?

Sam A tissue? Hang on. Where do you keep them?

Rosie I've no idea.

Sam I'll have a look. (*He goes into the kitchen and, finding no tissues, returns with the roll of paper towel. As he does this*) If it's any consolation—which of course it never is—I've just broken up a five-year relationship. I'm still getting over it. She went off with someone, too. Just walked out. I'm still getting over it...

Rosie (*not very interested*) Oh, yes?

Sam (*tearing off a piece*) Here. (*He passes it to Rosie*)

Rosie Thanks. (*She blows her nose*)

Sam I suppose, looking back, it was inevitable. She was sort of a childhood sweetheart, you know. Those things rarely work out long term, do they? I mean, we didn't get together, not then. Not as kids. We met up again much later—well, nearly ten years later—quite by chance—she'd been working abroad—she was a doctor—and, I don't know, it just seemed so right at the time. Us. We had the same sense of humour, the same interests. She was mad about opera, so was I. Well, most music really. And she was a fantastic tennis player. Far better than me. She could have turned professional. Only—medicine got in the way. But there's still this huge hole in my life. Frankly, I don't know if it will ever quite heal over. But you survive somehow, don't you?

Rosie Excuse me.

Sam Mmm?

Rosie I hope you don't mind me asking, but why are you telling me all this?

Sam I thought it might help.

Rosie Help?

Sam Just so you'd know you weren't alone. We all go through it. It's been the same for me, that's all I'm saying.

Rosie It's not the same at all.

Sam I'm sorry, I——

Rosie You breaking up with your girlfriend is totally different...

Sam Oh, come on... Don't start that...

Rosie It's not the same thing at all...

Sam I was only trying to be supportive, don't jump down my throat...

Rosie Listen...

Sam It's exactly the same. Some man walks off with my girlfriend, some woman walks off with your girlfriend. That's the only difference. The pain's the same. The hurt is just as real. That's all I'm saying. We may be different—differently oriented, if you like—but we still belong to the same species. We're both human beings, for God's sake.

Rosie I think you're mad.

Sam You want me to leave?
Rosie Yes, please.
Sam Right. (*He rises*) I tried. That's all, I tried. (*He indicates the kitchen roll*) Do you want any more of this?
Rosie No, thank you.
Sam I'll put it back. (*Rather crestfallen, he goes to the kitchen briefly*)

Rosie feels a bit guilty

Rosie Listen, I'm sorry, I... I'm sorry.
Sam Look, if this appears rude, I apologize, but have you always had this problem with your sexual identity?
Rosie (*outraged*) What?
Sam Because, frankly, in this day and age I think you're a little sad.
Rosie Do you? Do you now? Will you do me a favour? Just piss off.
Sam Right. Don't worry. I'm going. I just want to say this. I don't care if you're straight, I don't care if you're gay. To me, underneath we're all just people, darling. Now, if you want to see yourselves as a race apart, that's your problem and you can deal with it.
Rosie (*angrily*) What the hell are you talking about? You're completely and utterly howling. Go away!
Sam (*angry, too*) I'm going! Don't worry! I have better things to do with my life than stand here and be shouted at by narrow-minded lesbians.

Silence

Rosie I beg your pardon?
Sam Sorry. That was out of line. Sorry.
Rosie You think I'm gay?
Sam Aren't you?
Rosie No.

Pause

Sam Shall I come in again?
Rosie Why not?

Sam steps back into the front doorway

Sam Hi! I'm Sam. Sam Berryman. Flat 3B. From next door.
Rosie How do you do?
Sam I know we haven't met. I've been your neighbour for six months. (*He moves into the room*) What a lovely flat. (*At the open window*) Oh, look at

this view. Do you mind? Thank you. (*He steps out, looking to his right*) Oh, look, Tower Bridge! Terrific! (*He looks to his left*) Oh, look. The Dome! What's that you said? It isn't the Dome? Oh, I see. My mistake—I sense this is where it began to go wrong... For some reason you started crying. I'm sorry if it was anything I said. Maybe you were a major investor in the Dome. That would have done it.

Rosie Would you just shut up a minute!

Sam Certainly.

Rosie I am an actor. My agent has just phoned me to tell me that the role of Jane Eyre in a new BBC One classic serial—eight episodes—a role for which I am simply totally perfect in every respect and which they called me back to read for no less than five times—on every occasion like a dream—(*increasingly angrily*) and what's more which they practically promised me, on the fifth occasion, was definitely mine—the bastards have now decided to give to a six-foot beanpole with bright red hair and a Northern Irish accent they'd have trouble understanding in Londonderry.

Sam Oh, I see.

Rosie (*furiously*) As to my sexuality, that has absolutely nothing whatsoever to do with you and mind your own bloody business.

Silence

Sam Well, I'm glad we sorted that out.

Rosie (*surprised by her own outburst*) I'm sorry about your girlfriend.

Sam Thanks.

Rosie She just walked out on you?

Sam Yes.

Rosie For someone else?

Sam Right.

Rosie I'm sorry. (*Slight pause*) You must have been a bit to blame.

Sam What?

Rosie It couldn't have been all one-sided.

Sam Well, it was.

Rosie These things never are.

Sam This was.

Rosie You may see it that way. But that's because it suits you to. You just haven't asked yourself the right questions.

Sam What right questions?

Rosie Well—like—what was my part in this? What did *I* do wrong? Those sort of questions.

Sam I don't need to ask myself questions.

Rosie Yes, you do. Something you did caused her to react. Made her feel unwanted, inadequate. I don't know.

Sam No, you don't know. You don't know anything about it. She couldn't have been more wanted.

Rosie You drove her away somehow...

Sam (*irritably*) Why should it have been me, for God's sake?

Rosie Well, she must have had some reason. I mean, I've only been with you ten minutes and you're already driving me crazy...

Sam Oh, just take a jump in the river.

Rosie (*triumphantly*) There, you see!

Sam Goodbye.

Rosie Bye-bye!

Sam marches to the door and stops. A silence. He pulls himself together

Sam Shall I try coming in again?

Rosie I wouldn't bother.

Sam One more time. (*He composes himself*) Hallo. I'm Sam Berryman. You don't know me. I'm your neighbour from next door. I have only just clapped eyes on you and I appreciate you are probably not feeling at your very best but I just have to tell you that you are probably the most beautiful and attractive woman I have ever seen in my life and more than anything else, whatever your sexual preferences, I would dearly love to have dinner with you tonight. Please.

Rosie You are seriously deranged. Do you know that?

Sam Possibly.

Rosie Why on earth should I want to have dinner with you?

Sam (*shrugging*) Hunger...?

Rosie And everything else that that might entail?

Sam Dinner. That's all it entails. A little talk. Get to know each other better.

Rosie I know everything I need to know about you. You've already told me in the first five minutes.

Sam Oh, you'd be surprised. I have hidden depths.

Rosie Really?

Sam I have enormous plans for myself, you'd be amazed.

Rosie In a restaurant?

Sam If you like. Or we could eat at home.

Rosie I can't cook.

Sam I can.

Rosie One of your hidden depths?

Sam One of them.

Rosie Your place?

Sam Mine's a—bit of a mess. Since she left, I've rather let it ... you know...

Rosie I can imagine. How long's she been gone?

Sam Six years.

Rosie My God!
Sam Your place, then?
Rosie My—?
Sam I mean here?
Rosie Here?
Sam Yes.

Rosie is silent. Weighing it up

Say no. By all means. If you don't want to. I won't mind. I'll just go home, lie in the rubbish and cry myself to sleep. I'll get over it in a year or two. And I won't hold it against you, I promise.
Rosie (*after a pause*) OK.
Sam Here, then?
Rosie Just dinner.
Sam I'll buy the food and cook it here. Any preferences?
Rosie I eat most things.
Sam Pasta?
Rosie Fine. I'll buy the wine.
Sam Lovely.
Rosie Any preferences?
Sam I drink anything.
Rosie See you later then. Sam.
Sam Seven o'clock? Give me time to cook it?
Rosie OK.
Sam Oh, incidentally. Perhaps I should know your name.
Rosie My name?
Sam Yes. Something, you know, to call you. Unless it's a secret?
Rosie No. Joanna. Joanna Rupelford.
Sam (*looking at her somewhat strangely*) All right. See you later, then, Joanna. 'Bye.
Rosie (*softly*) 'Bye.

Sam leaves

The moment the door has closed, Rosie relaxes

Oh, my God! *Joanna?* What are you doing, Rosie? What the hell are you doing, girl?

The Lights fade to Black-out

SCENE 2

The same. It is now around 6.30 p.m. It is still light outside

Rosie is running slightly late. She enters dressed in a somewhat over-formal dress

The occasional river party boat passes noisily

Rosie (*not happy with herself*) ...this woman has the most extraordinary collection of clothes ... twenty-seven pairs of tights and one bra... I don't believe it... (*She studies herself*) This is way over the top. I can't wear this. He'll think we're going to the opera... Oh, look at the time... (*She grabs her bag and finds her make-up case. She sits at the table and does some simple additions*) Hallo, Joanna Rupelford ... so pleased to meet you. No, we've been in Cannes, actually. Came back yesterday. No, private jet. Reggie Heavily Bonking has one. Well, it's his father's, actually, Lord Bonking's. But since Lady Bonking passed away, he very rarely uses it. Except for bonking. Yes... Yes...

The doorbell rings

The bugger's early. Oh, God. Typical. This is doomed. This whole evening is doomed. (*She calls*) Just a minute! (*She hurriedly packs away her make-up and goes to answer the door*) You should know by now that it is fashionable to be five or—Oh.

It is not who she expects. It is Edna, in her forties, pleasant and smiling

Edna I'm so sorry to bother you, dear. Mrs Hall?
Rosie (*startled*) No.
Edna Oh. Not Mrs Hall?
Rosie No.
Edna Sorry, dear. I must have the wrong flat.
Rosie Afraid you have.
Edna Oh. How very strange. (*She tries to look past Rosie into the flat*)
Rosie (*awkwardly*) Well...
Edna I'm so sorry to have disturbed you, Miss—er——
Rosie Rupelford. Joanna Rupelford.
Edna (*flashing Rosie another smile*) Right, dear. Well, I'll sort it out, don't worry. 'Night.
Rosie 'Night. (*She closes the door*) God, I'll have to change again. I can't wear this, I feel like a call girl. (*She starts to remove the dress as she hurries*

to the bedroom) I can't believe I'm doing this. All for a chance of sex. I can't believe I'm doing it... Rosie, how can you have sunk so low...?

She goes off briefly to the bedroom

A river boat passes, pounding out loud music for excited party-goers

Rosie returns shortly, struggling into a new outfit, this time a black skirt and dark top

She goes into the kitchen. She takes a bottle of red wine from a carrier bag

Corkscrew? Corkscrew? Why can't this woman keep anything in a logical place? *(She realizes)* Bar! No, that's logical. *(She hurries to the bar and starts to open the bottle)*

The doorbell rings again. She takes a deep breath. She scans the room and switches off a light or so to create atmosphere

(Contemptuously) Rosie, this is so pathetic. You need to get laid this badly? Yes! Yes! Yes, I do! *(She goes to the hi-fi and surveys the CD rack. It contains just two CDs)* George Frederick Handel or Val Doonican. This woman is beyond belief! *(She puts on the Handel)*

It's the deceptively quiet opening to Zadok the Priest, *which Rosie obviously fails to recognize. The doorbell rings again*

She hurriedly goes and opens the front door to admit Sam. He, too, has changed his clothes but remains fairly casual. He has some cartons and carrier bags

Hi, sorry to keep you waiting.
Sam I'm not too early?
Rosie Spot on.
Sam Right.

They move to the kitchen

Rosie That our dinner?
Sam I've prepared what I could in advance. It shouldn't take long. I hope you're hungry.
Rosie Ravenous.
Sam Good. *(He sets down his packages)* You look very nice.

Rosie Thank you. So do you. Can I get you a drink?
Sam (*moving back into the sitting-room*) Sure.
Rosie Red wine?
Sam That'll do. Have you lost a bulb? It's a little dark, isn't it?
Rosie (*anxiously*) Is it too dark? I'll switch something on again.
Sam No, it's fine. Atmospheric. Great music, too.
Rosie Thank you. (*She starts to struggle with the corkscrew*)
Sam I can't believe you like Handel as well.
Rosie As well as what?
Sam This music. It's Handel.
Rosie Oh, yes. *This* is Handel, certainly.
Sam We have more and more in common.
Rosie We'll have to see, won't we?
Sam May I—?
Rosie (*handing him the bottle and corkscrew*) Thanks. You can have something else if you'd rather. I have—all sorts of things. I can hardly remember them all—(*reading off the stock from the bar*) Amaretto, Green Chartreuse, Calvados, Cointreau, Crème de Fraises, Crème de Bananes, Parfait Amour, Blue Curaçao, Triple Sec——
Sam (*finishing opening the bottle*) No, this'll be fine. You have an interesting selection of drinks.
Rosie Oh, I—pick them up when I'm touring around. You know.
Sam You do a lot of that?
Rosie I certainly do.
Sam Whereabouts do you go?
Rosie Oh, everywhere. Somerset. Everywhere.

He smiles at her. She smiles back. She starts to pour the wine with a certain flourish. The main choir on Handel's Coronation Anthem chooses this moment to kick in at full blast. Rosie slops the wine

(*Hurrying to the CD player to turn it down*) God! Sorry. (*She reduces the volume, apologetically*) Forgot it did that.
Sam *Zadok the Priest*. It does it every time. (*He moves to the kitchen*) Kitchen towel.
Rosie Still some left.

Sam returns with the roll of towel

Sam (*mopping the bar*) I was trying to remember if I'd ever seen you perform but I can't recall ... Joanna Rupelford. No.
Rosie No, well, I don't... I do mainly... (*She hands him a glass of wine*) Here.
Sam Thanks.

Rosie I mainly specialize in basically quite esoteric theatre work, you know...

Sam Uh-huh.

Rosie ...mainly to strictly limited ... mainly specialist audiences...

Sam Ah.

Rosie I don't particularly favour mainstream that much.

Sam Apart from *Jane Eyre*?

Rosie Apart from *Jane Eyre*. Which, of course, I didn't get. So it doesn't count.

Sam The Irish actress got it.

Rosie Right.

Sam They're going to regret that, aren't they?

Rosie Serve them right.

Sam Cheers.

Rosie Cheers.

They drink

Sam Remember this morning I said I thought you were the most beautiful woman I'd ever met?

Rosie (*casually*) Oh, did you? I seem to recall you said something like that, yes.

Sam Well. Right now I think you look even more beautiful.

Rosie (*nervously*) That's probably because I've switched most of the lights off.

Sam I don't think so.

They stare at each other

Rosie You certainly plunge in, don't you?

Sam Time's short. I'm already thirty-five.

Rosie Are you? I'm not.

Sam No.

They continue to stare at each other

Rosie You want to get cooking?

Sam Do I what?

Rosie Cooking? Do you want to start cooking?

Sam Oh, cooking. Yes, I'd love to cook.

Rosie Maybe you should? If time's that short?

Sam It's nearly all prepared. I'll just put the oven on. (*He drains his glass*) Interesting wine.

Rosie Thank you. What are we eating?
Sam Gnocchi.
Rosie What?
Sam Gnocchi.
Rosie K—N—O—C—?
Sam G—N—O—double C—H—I.
Rosie Oh.
Sam You said you liked pasta.
Rosie I thought you meant spaghetti.
Sam You'd prefer spaghetti?
Rosie No, I'm perfectly happy. I'm happy to try nooky.
Sam Gnocchi.
Rosie Gnocchi.
Sam (*staring at her*) I'll get underway, then. (*Sam goes into the kitchen and, during the following, fills a kettle. He then unpacks a few of his prepared ingredients*)
Rosie (*as soon as he has gone, attempting to cool herself*) Oh, Jesus! (*She hastily pours herself some more wine and swallows it in one*)

The phone on the desk rings. Rosie stares at it, uncertain whether to answer. It continues to ring

Sam (*from the kitchen*) Joanna!

Rosie continues to stare at the phone

Joanna! Are you going to answer that?
Rosie Oh! Yes. Of course. Probably only my mother. (*She goes to the phone and picks it up cautiously*) Hallo? (*She listens. Incredulously*) What? I'm sorry, I think you must have the wrong number. (*She hangs up. She calls to Sam*) Wrong number.
Sam Ah!
Rosie Do you mind if I put on some different music?
Sam It's your flat.

She switches off the Handel, takes out the disc. As she does so, another party boat goes by outside. The sound, again, of a thumping disco beat

(*Still in the kitchen, hearing this*) That's more like it.
Rosie That's from outside. On the river. Imagine being on board that. It must be deafening.

As the boat passes and fades she puts on the other disk, Val Doonican's Greatest Hits. *In a moment we hear "Paddy McGinty's Goat"*

Sam What the hell is this?
Rosie (*checking the sleeve*) Er—Val Doonican. "Paddy McGinty's Goat".
Sam This your sort of music, is it?
Rosie Can't get enough of it.
Sam (*somewhat sadly*) Ah. Well!

She listens briefly

Rosie On second thoughts, I think I've had enough of it. Tell you what, when
   I've had another glass of wine I'll sing to you instead.
Sam That'd be nice.
Rosie You'd be surprised. (*She takes the disc off again and goes back behind
   the bar. She is very slightly drunk already. A mixture of the wine and
   nervousness. She pours herself some more wine*)

Sam comes out of the kitchen

   More wine? (*She takes the bottle again*)
Sam Please. Do you happen to have a large saucepan? Or a big frying—?

Rosie manages to knock the cork off the bar. Sam catches it deftly

   —whoops!
Rosie Sorry.

Sam holds the cork for her to take

   (*Going to take it*) Thanks.

Suddenly the cork is no longer in Sam's hand. He has deftly palmed it

   (*Like a child, fascinated*) How did you do that?

The cork is made to reappear

   Hey!
Sam Now you see it, now you don't. (*He does a little vanishing-and-
   reappearing-cork routine*)

Rosie watches, spellbound

Rosie That's brilliant.

Finally, he hands her back the cork. She applauds

When did you learn to do that?

Sam Hidden depths. Ever since I was a kid. I belonged to this magic circle.
Used to write away for tricks. Spent all my pocket money on trick cards.
Vanishing coins. You know.

Rosie You should do it professionally.

Sam (*smiling*) I don't think so, somehow.

Rosie You should.

Sam I'm not that good. I do a bit at parties occasionally. For kids.

Rosie Kids?

Sam You know. At Christmas time, in hospitals, that sort of thing. Only as
a hobby.

Rosie (*now totally in love with him*) You entertain sick children in hospitals
at Christmas?

Sam When I have the time.

Rosie I adore magic. Well, that sort...

Sam Close-up magic?

Rosie I prefer it to all those women vanishing from boxes—getting sawn in
half.

Sam Well, that's technically illusionism. Sometimes it can be quite
impressive. It depends.

Rosie You do that as well?

Sam Not a lot. It takes up too much space. You need a very large garage to
store it and an endless supply of women to practise on.

Rosie Well. I'll volunteer.

Sam I don't think I'd want to make you disappear.

Rosie Not yet, anyway. You haven't discovered my hidden depths yet, have
you?

They smile at each other

No, I still think it's cleverer not to have to rely on lots of equipment, don't
you? Just doing it with your bare hands is much more satisfying. I should
imagine.

Sam stares at her

With magic.

Sam Oh, yes. I see what you mean.

Rosie I mean, I think it's cleverer if you can do it just with your hands. You
know—what do you call it——

Sam Manipulation?

Rosie Right. I mean, when you think of it. You—you, Sam—are able to give
people pleasure simply with what you can do with your hands. Aren't you?

Sam I suppose so, yes.

Rosie (*laughing nervously*) Now you see it, now you don't. It must be very satisfying.

Sam Right. I suppose it's the same for you.

Rosie Satisfying?

Sam I mean as an actor. You must give people a lot of pleasure, too, don't you?

Rosie Occasionally. Hopefully.

Sam That must be equally satisfying.

They stare at each other

I'd better get on in there.

Rosie Yes, or we'll never get round to——

Sam Eating.

Rosie No.

Sam moves back to the kitchen

This wine's going straight to my head, you know.

Sam (*returning to the kitchen*) Better go easy. The night is yet young.

Rosie Oh, I'll be fine. Don't worry. We thespians know how to hold our drink.

Sam I'm sure you do.

Rosie I'll have you know, I've survived first-night parties in Taunton. (*She pours herself another glass*)

Sam I'm impressed. (*He starts to sprinkle flour on to a chopping board*)

Rosie joins him in the kitchen and watches him for a moment

Rosie Can I help at all? I can't cook but I can chop for England.

Sam Don't think so. I've done most of it.

Rosie OK. (*She stands, feeling rather spare*) What are you doing there?

Sam I'm just going to roll out the gnocchi. I didn't bring pudding, I didn't know if we'd...

Rosie We can always improvise.

Sam True. Do you have that saucepan? Or a frying pan?

Rosie I don't know—I don't know if the one I have is still here. I'll have a look. (*She starts a vain hunt round, opening cupboards and drawers*) All this touring around. I see so many kitchens.

Sam You must do.

Rosie Dozens.

Sam Even though you don't cook.

Rosie (*triumphantly producing a pan*) What about this, then? This do?
Sam Perfect. No, I can see you don't do a lot of cooking, do you? This still
  has the label on.
Rosie Well, that's me. I can't cook but I adore the pans. Tell me, what's it
  like being an investment consultant? Is that what you said you did?
Sam At present.
Rosie At present? You don't plan to do that for ever?
Sam I certainly don't.
Rosie What do you want to do eventually?
Sam Oh, I have big plans for me.
Rosie Really?
Sam Big plans.
Rosie (*a little intrigued*) Want to talk about them?
Sam If you want to be useful, you could always lay the table.
Rosie Right. OK. (*She searches round again*) Now——
Sam (*indicating*) I think the cutlery's in that drawer there.
Rosie Yes, I knew. I knew that. (*She opens a drawer*)
Sam No, the second one down.
Rosie Yep. Just checking we had enough—of these wooden spoons.
Sam You appear to have dozens of them.
Rosie Yep. I'm mad about them as well. (*She takes some assorted cutlery
  from the second drawer and during the following lays it somewhat
  haphazardly around the table*) Hey! I just thought of a joke. Knocky,
  knocky…
Sam Sorry?
Rosie Knocky, knocky… You say, whosa there?
Sam Whosa there?
Rosie Emilio.
Sam Emilio who?
Rosie Emilio's always a nicer when there's a two of you to eat it. Boom-
  boom.

Sam shakes his head

  You get it? Knocky, knocky…
Sam Whosa there thissa time?
Rosie Harmonia.
Sam Harmonia who?
Rosie Harmonia here for the pasta.
Sam Knocky, knocky…
Rosie Whosa there *now*?
Sam Eustacia.
Rosie Eustacia who?

During the following Sam pours the boiling water from the kettle into the saucepan ready for the gnocchi

Sam Eustacia much longer making these terrible jokes, I throw you outta the window into the river, OK?
Rosie OK.

Sam places the saucepan on the stove to simmer. He locates an apron in a drawer and puts it on. He rinses his hands under the tap and dries them. He now takes the prepared gnocchi verde mixture out of its container and starts to mould it on the chopping board. Rosie watches him

Is thissa the gnocchi? Sorry. Is this the gnocchi?
Sam Right.
Rosie Can I have a go?
Sam Wash your hands.
Rosie Yes, Dad. (*She rinses her hands somewhat cursorily. She rejoins Sam at the board*) What do I do?
Sam Here. Do what I'm doing. Just roll a little of it out and when you've got it the right diameter then you just break a little off and roll it into little balls, you see——
Rosie Little balls...
Sam About two centimetres diameter...
Rosie Tiny. (*She starts to roll her portion of the mix*) Am I doing it right?
Sam You're doing just fine.
Rosie Tell me when it's long enough?
Sam A little more. Use both hands, just gentle, even pressure. That's it... Beautiful.
Rosie Can I taste a little?
Sam No, you wait till it's cooked.
Rosie What if I can't wait?
Sam You can wait. It always tastes better if you wait. Good. Now break a little off, like this—and just roll it between your palms... (*He demonstrates*)

Rosie copies him. They both roll their separate balls of dough but their eyes increasingly make contact

If your hands get a little sticky...
Rosie ...they're getting a little bit sticky...
Sam ...dip them in the flour ... like this... (*He puts his hands into the loose flour on the chopping board*)

Rosie does the same

24   FlatSpin

Rosie What do I do with my little ball when I've finished with it?
Sam You put it down on the board and you do it all over again...
Rosie Again?
Sam And again and again...
Rosie And again? I'll tell you something.
Sam What?
Rosie We'll be lucky if we get to eat this meal tonight...

Suddenly Sam grabs hold of her. She seizes him in turn. They kiss. No tender first exploratory kiss but the full works first time. He grabs her bottom and lifts her. She wraps her legs around his waist. Sam carries her to the table. They kiss the while

(*Coming up for air*) Oh, I needed that!
Sam (*likewise*) Oh, God...
Rosie Come on! Come on! Knocky! Knocky! (*She lands on the table*) Ah!
Sam You all right?
Rosie There's a fork sticking in my bum—don't worry, don't stop, it's fine, it's fine, it's fine...

Sam starts to lever off his shoes with his other foot, whilst simultaneously unfastening his trousers under the apron. Rosie, still on her back on the table, attempts the Houdiniesque feat of trying to take off her tights

Sam (*fumbling*) ...hang on ... just hang on...
Rosie (*wriggling*) ...why the hell did I bother to put tights on? Bloody control tights at that...
Sam Control tights?
Rosie (*breathlessly*) They're all she had in her drawer.
Sam (*his trousers down past his knees*) Whose drawer?
Rosie (*almost too far gone to think straight*) My—my mother's drawer.
Sam Your *mother*?
Rosie Help me. Help me get them off.
Sam You're wearing your mother's tights, for God's sake?
Rosie (*desperately*) Help me! Just get the bloody things off me.
Sam All right! All right! (*He struggles to pull off her tights. They are very tight tights and it's not easy, given the couple's current urgency*) Are these welded on or what?
Rosie Dear God, we're behaving like animals. We're no better than animals...
Sam Right, isn't it wonderful?

Loudly, the phone starts to ring on the desk. They freeze

Rosie Ignore it.
Sam You want to answer it?
Rosie Not now. Leave it.

The phone continues to ring

Sam Don't you have an answering machine?
Rosie I don't think I can have. No.

The phone rings on

Sam You'd better answer it.
Rosie Why should I answer it?
Sam Because it might be something important.
Rosie How could it possibly be important? How could it possibly?
Sam I don't know. Perhaps it's your mother. Demanding her tights back.
Rosie Oh, come on! I mean—it won't be. It can't be. It's far too late—for anything important. They'll ring off in a minute.

The phone rings on

Oh, sod it. (*Irritably, she struggles off the table. The top of her tights now down around her knees. She has Sam's handprints clearly outlined on the back of her skirt. She walks with difficulty to the phone*)

Sam, equally hobbled by his trousers, staggers a couple of steps before remembering. He hauls them up and holds them without refastening them

(*Moving to the phone*) We'll go in the bedroom, shall we?
Sam Right.
Rosie There's a perfectly good bed. Let's use it.
Sam I'll turn all this off. (*He goes to turn off the heat under the saucepan*)

Rosie picks up the phone. Sam, as he hears Rosie's call, stops in mid-task and comes into the sitting-room to listen

Rosie (*answering, crossly*) Hallo! (*She listens*) Look, I have told you before. This is the wrong number. Now go away. I'm very busy. (*She disconnects*) Bloody woman. Keeps ringing me.
Sam Who does?
Rosie Some woman. I think she's the same one who rang the doorbell earlier.
Sam (*suddenly quite alert*) When?
Rosie Earlier. Sounds like her.

Sam When was this?
Rosie Just before you arrived.
Sam You think it was the same one?
Rosie Sounded like her. Come on, let's go to bed.
Sam What did she say? When you answered?
Rosie She asked me the time, that's all?
Sam The time?
Rosie She's a lunatic. What's it matter? Come on, come to bed.
Sam She asked you the time?
Rosie Something like that. Can you give me the time? What's it matter?
Come on.
Sam Can you give me the time—or a time? Can you give me a time?
Rosie (*getting angry again*) Who cares?
Sam Please. Give it me exactly. You pick up the phone and then what?
Rosie I pick up the phone and I say hallo. And she says, can you give me—
a time, yes. It is *a* time. And I say bugger off and put the phone down.
Sam And this has happened twice?
Rosie Listen. I am going in the bedroom now, OK?
Sam And this was the same woman who was round here earlier, you think?
Rosie Yes, yes. I said. Are you coming or not?
Sam Can you describe her?
Rosie No.
Sam Did she say what she wanted?
Rosie She said she was looking for Mrs Somebody. I forget. Mrs Hall. Look,
I'm going in the bedroom, all right?
Sam OK.
Rosie You coming then?
Sam Sure.
Rosie You'd better. I'd hate to be you if I have to come out to get you.
Sam I'll just turn off the stove.
Rosie You have thirty-five seconds, all right? (*She marches to the bedroom,
still walking with difficulty*) It'll take me that long to remove these bloody
tights.

Rosie goes off to the bedroom

*As soon as she is gone, Sam locates his mobile phone and punches in a
memory code. He moves to the kitchen whilst it rings. He turns off the stove*

Sam (*after a pause*) D—five—double-one—six—three—zero. (*He waits*)
We have a possible breach. Yes… What, now?… *Now?* All right, all right,
all right. (*Angrily he disconnects*) Bugger! Bugger! Bugger!
Rosie (*off, calling from the bedroom*) You have exactly five seconds left!

Sam hesitates for a brief second, apparently torn between two options. Then, re-fastening his trousers, he moves swiftly to the front door and leaves, closing it behind him

(*Off, calling*) Sam!

Silence

Sam! I'm about to come out there and get you! (*She pauses*) Sam!

Silence

Right! I'm coming out.

Rosie enters from the bedroom. She has on a bathrobe and apparently very little else

Sam? (*She explores around*) Sam? (*Imagining some sort of game*) Sam! I don't believe this.

Another pleasure boat passes outside. Rosie goes out on to the balcony briefly

Sam! (*Bewildered*) Where the hell have you gone? Come on. This has to be a joke. SAM! (*Increasingly hurt*) He cannot have gone. I don't believe he could have done this to me. (*She goes to the front door and opens it briefly. She calls*) Sam! (*She realizes she is in no state of dress to go much further and closes the door again. Close to tears now*) He can't have gone. He can't have done. (*She sits, utterly miserable*) He *can't* have done. (*She starts to cry*) What did I do this time? What did I do this time? The bastard. Bastard... How could he do this to me? What a day! What a bloody awful, lousy, fucking day! (*She sits and cries for a while, rocking to and fro and hugging herself miserably. She just wants to die*)

Suddenly, the doorbell rings briefly. Rosie stops crying abruptly. She listens. The doorbell rings again. Rosie gets up and makes to run to the door

(*Checking herself*) Dignity! Dignity! (*She walks to the door more slowly. As she opens it*) If you think you can treat this place like a bloody hotel you're very—What?

Tracy, a woman of about Rosie's age, pushes past her and into the flat

Rosie turns, startled

What the hell do you think you're doing? You can't just walk in...

Tracy, without looking at Rosie at all, slides shut the window

Behind Rosie, Maurice, a man in his fifties, enters. He closes the front door, which causes Rosie to turn back startled

(*Seeing Maurice*) What is this?
Maurice (*pleasantly*) So sorry to intrude. This won't take a moment, I promise.
Rosie (*very indignantly*) What the bloody hell do you think you're doing?
Maurice Just a few seconds of your time. I promise.
Rosie Will you both get out of here? This is a private flat. Now get out, do you hear?

Tracy has moved a little closer to Rosie and is watching her attentively. Her face remains blank but there is about her a slightly tense, menacing air

Maurice Oh, yes, we're aware it's a private flat, don't worry. I'm sorry, we appear to have you at a disadvantage. Perhaps you'd care to pop a few clothes on before we have our chat...
Rosie I have no intention of doing anything of the sort. Now will you get out of my flat before I call the——
Maurice No, I don't think you want to do that. If you don't mind, Tracy there will come with you whilst you get dressed, just to make sure you don't try to jump out of the window or something... Tracy, would you mind accompanying Miss Rupelford...

Tracy steps forward and takes Rosie by the elbow. Rosie whirls round, furious and affronted

Rosie (*pulling away*) Will you take your hands off me at once? How dare you! Get out of my flat, both of you!

Tracy impassively steps in again to take her

I said take your hands off! (*She shoves Tracy away somewhat violently*)

Tracy responds rather swiftly to this by seizing Rosie's wrist and twisting her arm behind her. Before Rosie has time to respond, she has both her arms in a headlock

Bloody hell!

Maurice Now, Tracy, don't overreact, now, don't overreact! Just take Miss Rupelford to the bedroom, will you? Help her sort out something to wear.

Tracy propels Rosie to the bedroom

Rosie What are you doing? What the hell do you think you're doing?

Rosie and Tracy go into the bedroom

From off, a series of indignant squawks and squeaks from Rosie. It sounds as if Tracy may, rather forcibly, be helping her to get dressed

Maurice (*shaking his head disapprovingly, to himself*) Really, Tracy! You'll never make a lady's maid. (*He takes a walkie-talkie from his pocket and switches it on. Into the intercom*) 9-4. Check.
Walkie-Talkie (*distorted*) 9-4. Check.
Maurice (*into the intercom*) Access achieved. Welcome fair to moderate. Check.
Walkie-Talkie (*distorted*) 9-4. Need me there? Check.
Maurice (*into the intercom*) No, sit tight. Over and out. (*He switches off the set and tucks it away in his coat pocket*)

Another yell from Rosie, off. Maurice frowns and wanders to the window to watch a pleasure craft go by. The sound is muffled by the closed window. Maurice tuts disapprovingly. He goes to the kitchen and inspects the debris of the uneaten meal. He shakes his head again. He moves back into the room and inspects the CD player. He picks up the Handel disc and inspects it

(*Singing softly*) Zadok the priest and Nathan the prophet... (*He sits in the armchair and waits*)

In a moment, Tracy enters with Rosie. Rosie now wears a tracksuit and top and has her hands handcuffed behind her back

Oh, come along, Tracy, is all that strictly necessary?
Tracy (*sullenly*) She tried to punch me.
Maurice I'm sure you can cope with that, for God's sake, she's only two teapots high...
Rosie (*very angrily*) You are not going to get away with this. I am going to——
Tracy Shut up! (*She pushes Rosie down on the sofa and then sits beside her*)
Maurice Gently, Tracy, gently with Miss Rupelford. I think you're unfortunately in Tracy's bad books, Miss Rupelford. You weren't to

know, of course, but I think she feels you've rather stolen her thunder. But
we mustn't bear personal grudges, must we, Tracy? I've told you about that
before. Now, this won't take a moment, Miss Rupelford, as I say, just a few
simple questions and then we'll be on our way.

Rosie I'm not answering any questions while my hands are like this.

Tracy You'll do as you're fucking well told——

Maurice (*quite sharply, for him*) Tracy! Now I won't warn you again. All
right, Miss Rupelford, I'll tell you what I'll do. I'll offer you a deal. If I ask
Tracy to take those things off, will you agree to talk to me?

Rosie (*suspiciously*) Why should I do deals with you?

Maurice Well, I don't want to sound dispiriting, Miss Rupelford, but frankly
I don't think you've got an awful lot of choice at present, have you?

Rosie (*considering this*) What is it you want to ask me?

Maurice Oh, nothing too difficult, I promise.

Rosie (*after a second*) All right.

Maurice Tracy...

Tracy If she tries——

Maurice Tracy. You're being very naughty. Be a good girl now, or you'll
get a sound spanking, do you hear?

*Tracy scowls and produces the key. During the following she unfastens
Rosie's handcuffs and puts them away*

On occasions I have to be very firm with Tracy, you know, Miss Rupelford.
She's like that little girl in the poem. When she's good she's very, very
good, but when she's bad, she's quite perfectly horrible.

Rosie I can imagine.

Maurice Take my tip and try not to get too much on the wrong side of her,
will you? Thank you, Tracy.

Tracy sits on the sofa next to Rosie

Is that more comfortable, Miss Rupelford? Are you ready to talk to me,
now?

Rosie Not with her sitting here. I want her over there. (*She indicates towards
the windows*)

Tracy Listen, you just do as you're——

Maurice Tracy! Go and sit over there, that's a good girl.

*Tracy reluctantly goes to the desk. She sits, with her back to them, ostensibly
staring out of the darkened windows. One senses that she is, in fact, intently
watching the subsequent proceedings reflected in the glass*

Now then. Is that better, Miss Rupelford? I wouldn't try and make a run for it, by the way. You could no doubt lap me a couple of times but Tracy's got the speed of a champion whippet. Poetry in motion. Right, Miss Rupelford. To business. You've had a few phone calls tonight, I understand.

Rosie (*startled*) How do you know?

Maurice It's my business to know.

Rosie Who are you?

Maurice You also had a visitor, I understand.

Rosie What's it to do with you? I don't see why I should answer this——

Maurice Oh, Miss Rupelford, please——

Rosie —I'm not answering any of this, why the hell should I?

Maurice —don't make all this difficult and unnecessarily unpleasant.

Rosie I refuse to talk to you. Why should I? Get stuffed.

Maurice (*injured*) What happened to our deal?

Rosie Forget it.

Silence. Maurice stares at her, somewhat reproachfully. At the desk, Tracy breathes in and out deeply

Maurice There, you see. You've got Tracy going now. She's practically growling over there, Miss Rupelford. We don't want that, do we?

Rosie (*sulkily*) I don't care what she does.

Maurice Rupelford. What sort of name is that? Unusual, wouldn't you say? What is it, German? Danish? South African? Taiwanese?

Rosie No idea, I'm sure.

Maurice Oh, come along, now, Miss Rupelford, do brighten up. Try and contribute. You must be curious about your own name, surely?

Silence

Rosie (*softly*) That's not my name.

Maurice I beg your pardon? What did you say?

Rosie It's not my name.

Maurice Ah. I see. Well, that does alter the complexion of things, doesn't it? Are you sure about that?

Rosie Of course I am.

Maurice Only I understood this flat was leased by a Miss Rupelford. And when we first arrived a moment ago, you did claim to be her, did you not?

Rosie (*a little triumphantly*) No. I didn't! I never said I was her. You assumed I was her. I never said I was.

Maurice Perfectly true. But what you did say—and you will correct me if I'm wrong on this, won't you, Tracy— what you did say on I think two occasions, Miss Rupelford, was, get out of my flat. *My* flat. And since the flat is registered to a Miss Joanna Rupelford as sole lessee, somewhat understandably we assumed you to be her.

Silence

Now there are a couple of alternatives here, aren't there? Either you are Joanna Rupelford and you're trying for some reason to deceive us. Or you are not her but someone else entirely, in which case we could well jump to the other conclusion that you have no right to be here whatsoever but have been caught red-handed, breaking and entering someone else's property and impersonating the owner. Which one do you prefer?

Another silence

Rosie Are you the police?
Maurice Let's just say we're the good guys.
Rosie The good guys! You're joking!
Maurice Oh, you wait till you meet the bad guys. I promise you, they're really scary.

Pause

Rosie (*quietly*) My name is Rosie Seymore. I'm an actor. My uncle Sidney—Sidney Clarke—is the janitor here. He was in a car accident late yesterday, on his way back from holiday with my aunt. They're being kept in for observation. He phoned to tell me and asked me to inform the managing agents. I spoke to Mrs Sefton-Wilcox and she asked if I'd mind filling in for my uncle until he returned. Apparently his normal deputy is also away. I came round at lunchtime and I met with Mrs Sefton-Wilcox. That's all there is to it.
Maurice Well done. Pretty good so far, we're all ears, aren't we, Tracy? Carry on.
Rosie That's it.
Maurice One or two loose ends, surely? I mean, why aren't you busy janitoring? What are you doing in this flat?
Rosie I was—er—I was—watering the plants.
Maurice Oh dear! Suddenly the whole thing falls to the ground, doesn't it, Tracy? She was doing jolly well till then, too. Nearly convinced me.
Rosie It's the truth.
Maurice You've been doing a damn sight more than watering the plants, old thing. From the state of that kitchen I'd say you were midway through cooking a slap-up meal. The whole place is a positive shambles. What's the bedroom like, Tracy?
Tracy She's tried on half the wardrobe, had a bath and used the bed.
Rosie I have not used the bed. I merely turned it down.
Maurice Still sounds a far cry from watering plants, though. If you don't

mind my saying, I don't think the real Miss Rupelford's going to thank you for trying on her undies, is she?

Rosie Oh, God.

Maurice (*gently*) Come on, Rosie. Tell us the rest.

Rosie (*slowly*) I—I was watering the plants—this morning. When this man came to the door.

Maurice What man?

Rosie His name was Sam. Sam Berryman.

Maurice I see.

Rosie He—er... God, this is embarrassing—I didn't mean any harm—it was just that, like you did, he assumed that I was Joanna Rupelford, too. So I ... didn't—you know—disillusion him.

Maurice Why not?

No reply

Easy enough, surely? No, sorry, my name is Rosie. Simple enough.

Rosie I—liked him.

Maurice Liked him?

Rosie Yes, you know—I wanted—wanted—wanted to get to know him.

Maurice So why didn't you get to know him as Rosie Seymore? Ask him next door to the pub? They serve an excellent pint.

Rosie I don't know. I thought he'd be more impressed if he thought I owned this flat. It was only going to be a one-night thing. He'd probably have found out in the morning.

Maurice And where is this man now?

Rosie He—just walked out.

Maurice Why did he do that?

Rosie (*unhappily*) I've no idea.

Maurice Why on earth should he walk out? It sounds to me as if he was on to a sure thing, wasn't he?

Rosie Oh, for God's sake. Just leave me alone. That's all there was to it. Either arrest me or go away. If you don't believe me, check with him.

Maurice We'll need to. Where does he live? Do you know? Did he tell you?

Rosie Yes. Next door. He lives in the flat opposite.

Silence

Maurice Does he now?

Rosie Yes. You can check. He may be out at present, but that's where he lives.

Pause

He does.

Pause. She looks at Maurice

He doesn't?

Pause

Oh, God. (*She starts to cry again*) I'm sorry. I've had this most terrible day...

Maurice (*sympathetically*) Oh dear, poor old thing. This chap sounds to me what my dear late mother would call a bit of a cad.

Rosie He was a lousy, deceitful, lying bastard.

Maurice That's another way of putting it, I suppose. (*He proffers a neatly folded handkerchief*) May I?

Rosie (*taking it from him*) Thank you. (*She blows her nose, then offers it back to him*)

Maurice Now, Rosie—(*refusing the handkerchief*)—no, no, do hold on to it, you may be needing it again in a moment—now, Rosie. We're in a bit of a quandary here, you and I. This innocent if somewhat illegal romantic escapade of yours has rather upset the Cox's Pippins, you see——

Rosie What?

Maurice You've rather buggered things up, old thing.

Rosie How do you mean? I'll clean things up. Miss Rupelford need never know. There's no harm done, surely?

Maurice I'm afraid there's been an awful lot of harm done, Rosie.

Rosie Who's going to tell her?

Maurice Nobody's going to tell her, certainly.

Rosie Well, then.

Maurice No-one's going to tell her because there's no such person as Joanna Rupelford.

Pause

Rosie There isn't?

Maurice Not until you laid claim to the title. Dear Joanna was simply a somewhat painstakingly concocted fictional character. True, we had intended to—bring her to life—but only at the point she was needed.

Rosie Needed for what?

Maurice Unfortunately you appear to have stepped into her shoes. How do they put it in your line of business? The understudy's gone on instead of the principal. If we're not careful, we'll have people demanding their money back.

Rosie But who is the principal, then?

A slight pause

Tracy Me.
Rosie Ah.
Maurice Yes. So you can understand why Tracy's a bit miffed, can't you? She's been rehearsing this for weeks. It was to be her big chance. Her starring role. To add insult to injury you've even tried on most of her costumes.
Rosie Were those your tights?
Tracy (*hostile*) Yes.
Rosie Well, I didn't know, did I?
Maurice No excuse in law that, you know.
Rosie Well, she can still do it. She can carry on with it, can't she? She can still be Joanna Rupelford?
Maurice Hardly.
Rosie Why not?
Maurice Rosie, the play is halfway through. You can't suddenly switch leading ladies. The punters will get suspicious. Who the hell's this, they'll cry? Who's this Tracy girl who's suddenly entered down centre in the middle of things? Bring back Rosie! We want Rosie! No, Rosie, I fear you're in too deep. I think the only solution to this, like it or not, is that you're going to have to carry on till the curtain.
Tracy You've got to be joking!
Rosie He certainly has.
Maurice There's an awful lot of time and effort gone into this, you know.
Rosie Too bad. (*She suddenly gets up*) Look, I'm going home. I've had enough of this.
Tracy (*also on her feet, sharply*) Sit down, you!
Rosie Get out of my way!
Tracy Sit down, or I'll break every finger you've got.

Rosie stares at her

Maurice (*softly*) I think she's probably exaggerating a weeny bit, Rosie, but I wouldn't put her to the test.

Rosie sits. Tracy now sits next to her

Rosie (*looking at them both, a little more frightened now*) You're not the police at all, are you?
Maurice Never said we were, old thing. Now. Can we rely on you, Rosie? Come on, we really could do with a spot of help here, you know.

Rosie Why should I help you?

Maurice (*hopefully*) Patriotism?

Rosie (*drily*) Ha-ha!

Maurice (*shrugging*) Well, worth a try, wasn't it? How about immunity from prosecution, then? From breaking and entering? Wanton damage to property? We could probably put a pretty good case together between us, couldn't we, Tracy? Get you six to nine months in a nasty women's prison full of big rough girls. You wouldn't like that, surely, Rosie?

Rosie You're not going to frighten me. I'm reporting this to the authorities.

Maurice I should. They'll be very pleased to see you. Save them hunting for you, won't it?

Rosie I'll report it to someone. I'll report it to Equity.

Maurice My God! We hadn't reckoned with that, had we, Tracy? Well, I suppose, as a last resort, we could always try Tracy's way. Not an ideal solution. A leading lady with both her hands in plaster, but we could give it a whirl if you like. What do you think, Tracy?

For the first time Tracy looks at Rosie and smiles. It is somewhat unnerving

Want to have a rethink, Rosie?

Rosie No.

Maurice You're not going to help us?

Rosie No bloody way.

Maurice (*studying her*) I must say, I rather admire you. You've got a lot of guts.

Tracy Be all over the bloody carpet in a minute——

Maurice (*sharply*) That'll do, Tracy.

Rosie I'm standing up now and I'm going home to my aunt and uncle's flat, all right? If you want to stop me, you're going to have to use force.

Nobody moves. Their bluff is called. Rosie stands up

Maurice Rosie, would you mind just—just giving me one more moment? I need to make a quick phone call? Would you do that? Please? Please.

Rosie You'd better be quick.

Maurice I promise. Tracy, behave yourself. Lay a finger on Rosie, I'll take my belt off to you. (*He smiles at Rosie*) Just our little private joke. Don't mind us. (*He takes out his mobile and wanders towards the bedroom. Into the phone*) Hallo. I think we need to call up the infantry. Yes. Right away, please. Yes. OK… Uh-huh… Yes…

Maurice wanders off, still listening

Rosie and Tracy sit in silence for a moment

Rosie (*at last*) What exactly have you got against me?

Tracy (*regarding Rosie with loathing*) Do you know how long I trained for this job? Six months. I did advanced assault courses, weapons training, unarmed combat and endurance tests; I underwent round-the-clock interrogation, sleep-deprivation and psychological torture. I got dunked in cold water and sat in a freezing bloody cell with a black bag on my head for three days with no food, listening to nothing but a high-pitched whistling noise. Then somebody came along and kicked the shit out of me just for the hell of it. I underwent all that in return for a promotion and fifty lousy quid a month increase and then along comes a pissing little amateur like you and takes it all away from me. How should I feel exactly?

Rosie (*with growing passion*) OK. I also trained for two years in drama school. To become a professional actor. I did movement, voice training, fencing, stage fighting and basic mime. I spent most of my time there crying in the loo, having been humiliated by so-called visiting directors who couldn't get a job in the proper theatre so decided to take it out on us kids and by a load of bored tutors who couldn't give a monkey's fuck. All in all, I was laughed at, humiliated and made to feel a complete and utter uncoordinated prat. I was told I was unattractive, too short, that my ass was too big—and by one teacher that I had the acting talent of a gnat. Never mind, despite that, I hung on in. I stuck it out, finished the course and entered the glorious world of professional theatre where I have been for two years. Twenty-two months of that I have been out of work, occasionally auditioning and being told by casting directors that I wasn't quite what they were looking for, darling. The other two months I spent wearing a bloody nylon-fur skin and a rabbit's head that would make your black bag seem like paradise. I slept in a transit van with six others, including a stage manager with an unbearable foot problem, and all for twenty quid less than the recommended Equity minimum and no subsistence. And all because I knew inside me that one day my break would come. And it did come and I was on the verge of real stardom and it all suddenly seemed worthwhile and then along comes this lanky, talentless, six-foot, toothsome redhead straight from drama school and just snatches it all away from me. So, how do you think that feels, eh?

Silence

Tracy (*impressed, despite herself*) Jesus.

Rosie May I go home now, please?

Tracy (*with a glance towards the bedroom*) Go on, then.

Rosie Thank you. (*She gets up and walks to the front door a little unsteadily*)

Tracy, still seated, watches her go without moving

As Rosie reaches the door, it opens and Sam is standing there

Rosie gapes at him

Sam (*somewhat sheepishly*) Hi.
Rosie You came back?
Sam I couldn't keep away.
Rosie Why? Why did you walk out, Sam?
Sam I'm sorry. Forgive me? (*He holds out his arms*)
Rosie (*embracing him and clinging tightly, muffled*) Just take me home. Take me home, please. These bloody people, they're trying to...
Sam (*rocking her gently*) OK. OK. I'm here now.

Tracy watches them, impassively

Maurice enters from the bedroom, putting away his mobile phone

Rosie (*still clinging to Sam*) Get me out of here, please, Sam. (*She is suddenly aware that Sam is not moving. She pulls away slightly*)
Maurice Just sit down again for a minute, will you, Miss Seymore?

Rosie looks from Sam to Maurice to Tracy then back to Sam. Alarm bells are starting to ring in her head

Rosie Sam?
Sam Do as he says, Rosie.
Rosie (*the truth dawning, softly*) Oh, my God. What a day!

She continues to stand as the Lights fade to Black-out

CURTAIN

ACT II

SCENE 1

The same. A few minutes later

Rosie is sitting dejectedly. Maurice, Sam and Tracy stand watching her

Silence

Sam (*at length*) Rosie?
Rosie Why should I ever do anything for you?
Sam If you could only try and——
Rosie (*rising*) Forget it. I'm changing back into my own clothes and then I'm going to phone for a taxi. (*To Tracy, moving off*) You want to come and watch me change, you're welcome.

Rosie goes off to the bedroom

Silence. None of them moves

Maurice Tracy, give us a moment, will you, please?

Tracy starts to move towards the bedroom

No, not in there. Leave her alone. The woman's had quite enough for one night. Go and wait in the hall there.
Tracy (*going, turning*) Do you want me to——
Maurice (*sharply*) I said wait in the hall!

Tracy goes, sulkily

Maurice, although he is trying to contain himself, is clearly very angry

Well, you've certainly cocked this up, haven't you, boy? This is all down to you, you realize that?

Sam shrugs, sulkily

Never could keep the bloody thing in your trousers, could you?

Sam (*muttering*) This wasn't like that at all.

Maurice What was it, then. True love?

Sam I—I like her.

Maurice Delighted to hear it. Sooner you marry her the better, then. Because you'll have all the time in the world for your honeymoon, I'll tell you that much. You're out of this department as of now.

Sam stands miserably

When I first recruited you, I had big hopes for you, son. You were quick, you were intelligent, you had everything going for you. You could have gone right to the top, Sam. Nothing could have stopped you. Nothing. Except your own total lack of personal self-control. What the hell did you think you were playing at? Eh?

Sam All I did was——

Maurice All you did was wreck eighteen months' work and nearly a million quid's worth of operation. That's all you've done, boy. All because you couldn't control yourself. Had to be the bloody magician producing things out of his trousers. What the hell were you doing in here in the first place?

Sam I heard her in here, I thought I'd...

Maurice Check her out. That's what the gear is for, Sam. That's why we have cameras in the lavatory and mics in the spin dryer. So we don't need to come near the place until we need to. It's called surveillance, Sam. You sit on your ass next door and you listen and you watch. And you regularly report in. You do not swan in here at the first sign of available totty and start cooking her bloody tagliatelle.

Sam Gnocchi.

Maurice What?

Sam Nothing.

Maurice paces about, quite agitated

Maurice I don't know what we're going to do, Sam, I really don't. Have I now got to go back and tell them the whole thing's blown? That's going to look wonderful, isn't it? I retire in two years, do you realize that? Nothing like going out in a blaze of glory, is there? Well, there goes the bloody Christmas bonus for a kick-off.

Silence

Sam It might still be running.

Maurice Running? How can it possibly be running? That woman's not going to keep coming back, is she? She's called once, phoned twice. They may be villains but they're not idiots, Sam. I think she may have gathered by now that everything here is not as it should be.

Sam We still have one card.

Maurice What?

Sam Rosie.

Maurice I think you'll find she's what we call a busted flush, Sam. You may have gathered from your brief reunion that she is not in the mood to co-operate. Neither I at my most charming nor Tracy at her least alluring could budge her an inch.

Sam I could try, if you like.

Maurice What do you propose to do? Cook her an omelette?

Sam I could try talking to her. She might listen.

Maurice If I were her, I'd punch you in the eye.

Sam I could try.

Maurice (*sighing*) Nothing to lose, have we? Apart from our jobs, our pensions, our reputations, our friends—possibly our lives—nothing momentous.

Pause

You've got five minutes. Then I'm pulling everyone out. We've got three teams out there, you know. Living on a diet of fast food and peeing into plastic bags. God knows what the overtime bill is. I shudder to think. Five minutes. Understood?

Sam Right.

Maurice I must say, I don't fancy your chances. She's a feisty little thing.

Maurice goes out of the front door

Sam sits thoughtfully

In a moment, Rosie comes from the bedroom. She has on her original clothes. She sees Sam but chooses to ignore him. She stops at the desk and rummages through her bag for her mobile phone

Sam (*softly*) Rosie...

Rosie ignores him. She trawls through her stored numbers

Could I just say one thing...?

Rosie keys in the number

Please. (*He rises and moves to her*) Rosie!

Rosie (*very coolly*) Would you keep away from me, please. (*Into the phone*) Hallo... Yes, could I have a taxi immediately? ... Yes, it's St Mark's Wharf, 177 Wapping High Street. Yes. Flat 3C. Seymore. Yes. Well, as soon as you can, please. (*She disconnects, and moves towards the front door*)

Sam Rosie...

Rosie We have nothing to say, do we?

Sam Just till the cab comes. Sit down a second.

Rosie lingers but does not sit

First, I'd like to say—I know how you feel. Yes, there was deception. I didn't—I didn't tell you the whole truth about myself. Why I was here—what was going on. But I think you have to admit, there was deception on both sides. Wasn't there? I mean, you deceived me, too.

Rosie What are you talking about?

Sam You tried to pass yourself off as Joanna Rupelford. Make me believe this was your flat, didn't you?

Rosie But you knew I was lying. From the very start, you knew it wasn't true, didn't you? You knew who owned this flat. That there wasn't really a Joanna Rupelford. You knew all along.

Sam Yes, but—does that make it less of a lie? Just because the person you're telling the lie to knows it's a lie. It's still a lie. The intention's the same.

Rosie Are you saying this is my fault?

Sam No, of course not. I'm trying to say to you, that despite the fact that we both lied to each other—I think we both lied for the same reason. To try and—create time for each other. To know each other a little. To get closer. And I don't want to lose that. I really don't. What I feel for you is very important to me. That's all. I don't want to lose you. I'm asking you to try and forgive me, Rosie. And to give us a chance to have more time together. That's all.

Rosie takes this in

Rosie I think you're full of shit, Sam.

Sam (*meekly*) Then you'll have to forgive that as well.

Rosie You need to understand this about me. Every single man I've ever met, that I've ever had a relationship with, has finished up using me, taking advantage and eventually walking out on me. And I am now twenty-six years old and just a little sick of being walked out on, that's all. This time I am walking first, Sam. I mean, yes, in truth, you are somewhat unique. You're certainly the first man who's walked away *before* we've been to

bed together—but all in all you're just another bloody man and I've had
it up to here with them, Sam, I really have, I'm sorry. No more. Finish. To
hell with all of you. God, I'm so pissed off I've half a mind to go out there
and proposition Tracy.

Sam Sit down. Just till your cab comes.

Rosie sits away from him

There's a way out of this. For us. It needn't all finish. If you'll give it
another go, I don't intend to walk out on you ever again.

Rosie Ah, now. No-one's ever said that to me before. Golly, he must he
telling the truth, surely. Hey, what do you know? More hidden depths.

Sam It is the truth, for God's sake. Listen, if you go through with what they
want, carry on pretending to be Joanna Rupelford—we can not only get out
of it together—but we can have a future. I promise you.

Rosie What are you talking about? *We* can get out of it? I was never in it.

Sam You are in this just as deep as I am, Rosie, and unless we go through
with it, neither of us is going to get out. I know it's through no fault of your
own but you have to believe that. At present, you need me just as much as
I need you. Trust me.

Rosie Trust you? Trust you?

Sam Please.

*Rosie looks at him. She rises abruptly, picks up her bag and leaves by the
front door, slamming it behind her*

*Sam sits frustratedly. A pause. There is the sound of a front-door key in the
lock. He rises*

Rosie returns, drops her bag, puts down her keys and stands for a second

Rosie God, I'm doing it again. I can feel it.

Pause

What do you want?

Sam Thank you.

Rosie Is it dangerous?

Sam There'll be someone with you all the time.

Rosie You?

Sam No. Someone—better suited than me. Who can protect you properly.

Rosie Protect me?

Sam If need be.

Rosie Great. Well, anyone but Tracy.

Sam It won't be Tracy.

Rosie What is it you want me to do?

Sam That woman—the one who called here earlier tonight—her name is Edna Stricken. She's a courier.

Rosie (*drily*) Travel agent, is she?

Sam No. Not that sort of courier, she——

Rosie No, I think I've guessed what sort of courier.

Sam She'll be here with a briefcase full of merchandise. You'll need to examine it—we'll show you how to do that—then once you're satisfied, you'll give her another case which contains the money to pay for it. She leaves. End of story.

Rosie That all?

Sam That's all you need to do.

Rosie Why can't Tracy do that?

Sam Because this woman's already identified you as Joanna Rupelford. You're the one she's expecting to meet. She smells a rat she'll turn and run. And we'll lose her.

Rosie This is a—what do you call it—a sting.

Sam Sort of thing. Our real interest is what happens after she leaves here. We need to follow the trail back. Wherever Edna leads us.

Pause

Of course, she may already have bolted. Depends if she was put off when she phoned.

Rosie I wasn't particularly forthcoming.

Sam No, but she doesn't know why that was, does she? You may have had someone here you didn't want to talk in front of, for instance.

Rosie I did.

Sam Exactly.

Rosie So we wait and see if she phones again? Or not?

Sam All we can do.

Rosie What happens if she does?

Sam You answer it. And tell her to come on round.

Rosie I see.

Sam You'll do it, then?

Rosie Oh, God, Sam. If you're two-timing me on this, I swear I will come after you with the biggest most pointed knife. Glenn Close knew no greater fury…

Sam I promise. (*He reaches for her, tentatively*)

She moves close to him

Rosie (*nuzzling up to him*) Have we got time to go in the bedroom?
Sam Probably not just at present.

They remain as they are until they hear the sound of a key scraping in the front-door lock

Rosie (*alarmed, softly*) What's that?
Sam (*rising swiftly, quietly*) Sssh! Keep away from the door!

Sam draws back into the kitchen slightly. Rosie ducks behind the furniture

The front door opens. Maurice and Tracy enter. Maurice, sensing trouble, pushes Tracy ahead of him

Sam and Rosie emerge

Maurice Hallo, there. What fun! Playing hide-and-seek now, are we? Miss Seymore, I understand you've agreed to help us. Thank you so much. I'm eternally grateful.
Rosie How did you know—?
Maurice I was just next door. I couldn't help overhearing.
Rosie My God! (*To Sam*) It's a good job we didn't, isn't it?
Maurice What? You mean in the bedroom? Oh no, I wouldn't try anything in there. It's like Vista Vision. Be on late-night Channel 5 before you know it.

Silence

Well. Shall we sit down? All we can usefully do now is wait and hope.

They all sit

I do just want to reassure you, Rosie, if this all goes ahead that at no stage will you be in any sort of danger. This is a simple transfer. A hand-over operation. No need for heroics. We'll take it over the moment the woman leaves this flat. As far as you're concerned, that's the end of it. You'll probably need to sign the odd confidentiality agreement, that sort of thing. But I can see no reason why we need ever bother you again after tonight.
Sam She'll get expenses, though?
Maurice (*blankly*) Expenses?
Sam Expenses.
Maurice Yes. I suppose so, yes. What expenses?
Rosie All my expenses.

Maurice (*glaring at Sam*) Yes, of course. I daresay we can swing that. Probably.

Silence

Rosie Is she dangerous, then? This woman?
Maurice What, Edna? Good Lord, no. Edna's an old softie. A pussy cat. Run-of-the-mill courier. Turn and bolt soon as look at you.
Tracy (*murmuring*) That's not what I was told. They told me she'd got a record of violence and——
Maurice Tracy, old love, would you like to pop out into the hall for a second? Refresh the make-up, powder the nose, there's a good girl.

Tracy gets up, scowling

Thanks so much.

Tracy goes out of the front door

(*To the others*) First rate at her job but socially an absolute disaster. I made the dreadful mistake of taking her to the Danish Ambassador's Ball last Christmas. Nearly severed diplomatic relations altogether.
Rosie So this woman is dangerous.
Maurice Well ... only if roused. But then we all have a bit of a temper, don't we? But if you don't annoy her, as I say, Edna's a pussy cat. Utter pussy cat. And you will have back-up, remember, Rosie. I'm putting one of my best chaps in here specifically to guard you. Ex-SAS, tough as an old-fashioned gas cooker. Nothing'll get past him. OK?
Rosie (*still a little doubtful*) Yes.

Pause

Maurice Of course, none of this would have happened if I hadn't given Tracy time off to go and bury her mother.

A pause. The phone rings. They stare at it

Tracy enters swiftly

Rosie (*rising*) Shall I—?
Maurice Just a second. Couple more rings. You know what to say?
Rosie Come on round?
Maurice That'll do. Answer it now. Be brief.

Rosie answers the phone

Rosie Hallo ... yes, it is... Yes. All clear... Come on round... 'Bye. (*She rings off*) She'll be here in forty minutes.

Maurice Well done, Rosie. Well done. (*With satisfaction*) All right, everybody. It's showtime.

The Lights fade to Black-out

SCENE 2

The same. Thirty minutes later

The kitchen has been tidied a little

Maurice and Sam are standing nervously. Tracy with her walkie-talkie is doing a last-minute check on the concealed mics. Rosie is sitting at the desk. She has changed back into a rather svelte evening outfit to play out her scene with Edna. She is applying some make-up, occasionally pausing to watch Tracy at work

Tracy (*flatly*) ...window mic... testing—1-2-3-4-5...

Walkie-Talkie (*distorted*) Check.

Maurice Where's Tommy? He should be here by now.

Tracy Desk... testing—1-2-3-4-5... (*During the following she moves to the dining area*)

Walkie-Talkie (*distorted*) Check.

Sam He was apparently in the middle of his break, sir.

Maurice Wonderful! This whole bloody country's on one long break if you ask me.

Tracy Dining table ... testing—1-2-3-4-5...

Walkie-Talkie (*distorted*) Check.

Maurice We never had all these breaks. We worked right through till we finished.

Tracy Kitchen ... testing—1-2-3-4-5...

Walkie-Talkie (*distorted*) Check.

Maurice Sorry, everybody. Had to call the Normandy landing off—the chaps are on their break.

Tracy (*into the walkie-talkie*) Cameras OK? (*She waves her arms at the walls and ceiling*)

There appear to be a couple of cameras in each area

Maurice (*watching Tracy with admiration*) God, look at that girl move. Poetry in motion.

Tracy All working?

Walkie-Talkie (*distorted*) Working.

Tracy That's the lot, then.

Walkie-Talkie (*distorted*) Thank you.

Tracy (*to Maurice*) All checked out, sir.

Maurice Thank you, Tracy. Better get next door. See if you can find out what's happened to Tommy.

Tracy I think he's on his break.

Maurice (*rather irritably*) Yes, so I gathered.

Tracy moves to the front door

> *She opens it to be faced with Tommy, a thickset man in a tracksuit. He carries a briefcase*

Tommy Oh hallo, beautiful. How's gorgeous Tracy then?

Tracy (*with ill-disguised contempt*) Get stuffed.

> *Tracy goes out, closing the door*

Tommy Reporting for duty, sir.

Maurice Where the hell have you been, Tommy?

Tommy Constitutional, sir.

Maurice Is that what it's called?

Tommy Anticipating I might be required for protective duties, sir. I took the opportunity to have a good workout, sir.

Maurice Don't give me all that bullshit, Tommy, you've been rogering some tart senseless, haven't you?

Tommy Very few of those down this way, sir. It's a bit of a yuppie zone. Strictly amateurs only.

Maurice Never stopped you, did it? Rosie, this is Tommy Angel who will be looking after you. Tommy, this is Miss Seymore who is seconded to us for this operation. I want you to look after her as if your life depends on it. Because I can assure you that indeed it does. Understood?

Tommy Sir. Good evening, ma'am.

Rosie 'Evening.

Maurice And insofar as this operation is concerned, you treat her as your superior officer, you hear? You do as she tells you. You respect her every wish and whim and if you lay so much as an exploratory digit upon her, you are as good as dead, Angel. You understand that?

Tommy Sir! Wouldn't dream of it, sir!

Maurice Is that the money?

Tommy Sir!

Maurice Give it here, then. Rosie, this is your case. It's got one or two readies in here. It's all genuine notes, they'd know immediately if they weren't, so guard it like a hawk. Better check it.

Rosie I trust you.

Maurice Don't trust me. Check it. First rule of this game, Rosie. Trust no-one. Check everything. Guns, parachutes, explosives, suitcases. Check them all. Because when the chips are down, the plonker who screwed up is going to be in the public bar in the King's Road whilst you're lying flat on your face in a field in Bosnia. Always check.

Rosie Right. (*She opens the case. It is full of high-denomination notes*) My God!

Maurice It's all there I trust, Tommy? Haven't spent any on tarts, have you?

Tommy Wouldn't dream of it, sir.

Maurice (*to Rosie*) Satisfied?

Rosie Seems OK to me.

Maurice Right. Put it away then, Sam.

Sam Right, sir.

Whilst Sam demonstrates to Rosie, Maurice goes out of the front door. Tommy wanders off to the bedroom

Rosie (*to Sam*) Do you all call him sir?

Sam Only when we're operational. Now. You keep the case in here. Look. (*He runs his fingers under the edge of the coffee table and the top pops up slightly on a concealed spring*) See? Can you feel the catch just under the rim here?

Rosie Yes? Why all this?

Sam Makes it a little more convincing. Only an idiot would leave all that money lying about before they'd checked the merchandise. Your case fits in here. See?

Rosie Right.

Sam Then you just press down the lid again and it locks. Just a little box of tricks. Not foolproof, but it would take them some time before they found it.

Rosie Ingenious. Did you make it?

Sam (*modestly*) Abracadabra. Guilty.

Rosie Clever. More hidden depths.

Sam More hidden depths. So. Check the merchandise, like we showed you. And then, and only then, open this and let her see the money. Finally, when she's happy, put her case away in here. All clear?

Rosie All clear.

Maurice appears briefly at the front door

Maurice Better clear out now, Sam. Very nearly time.

Maurice goes

Sam (*softly to her*) Will you be all right?
Rosie I hope so.
Sam We won't be far away. Tommy's a good man. He's an idiot but he knows what he's doing. You'll be fine. Take care. (*He kisses her lightly*) I love you.
Rosie (*startled*) What?
Sam Sorry. I didn't mean to say that. Sorry. Not the time, is it? 'Bye.

Sam goes out of the front door

Rosie (*following after him, to herself*) What did he say?

Maurice enters briefly

Maurice Cheerio, Rosie. Good luck. Think of it as a first night. Pull this off, you never know, I might even send you a bunch of flowers. See you in a minute. What is it you say? Beginners, please.
Rosie (*blankly*) Yes, sir.

Maurice goes out

Rosie decides to get into character for her role as Joanna

In time, Tommy wanders back on. He nods

Tommy Just you and me then, eh?
Rosie (*a little warily*) Yes.

Tommy does a few limbering up movements

Tommy (*indicating his stomach*) You want to get a feel of that?
Rosie What?
Tommy (*patting his stomach again*) This. Like a fucking iron bedstead, this is.
Rosie Great.
Tommy Want to feel?
Rosie No, thank you.

Tommy (*punching himself hard*) Iron. (*He punches himself again*) Like steel. That's all exercise, that is.

Rosie Would be.

Tommy This woman tries anything with you, I'll bring her down like that. Break her spine, bring her down. (*He gestures*) Like that. Seven years SAS.

Rosie Wow.

Tommy They don't hang around.

Rosie So I've heard.

A pause. Tommy jiggles around restlessly

What are you in now? MI5?

Tommy MI5. You must be joking. Never in a month of Sundays.

Rosie No?

Tommy Wouldn't catch me there. More sense than that.

Rosie Dangerous, is it?

Tommy Dangerous? No, it's not dangerous. It's the pay. It's terrible. They're as mean as buggery. I tell you, I used to have a brother-in-law that was in '5. They flew him out over Easter—he missed the whole of Easter for covert operations—know what I'm saying?—they flew him out to the Middle bloody East, Operation Desert Storm going on all around him, Arabs taking shots at him, all of that—he gets back by the skin of his teeth—and he puts in, you know, naturally, for his Bank Holiday overtime— Good Friday, Easter Monday. Do you know what they told him? You are seriously not going to believe this. They told him he couldn't claim because he wasn't technically speaking in a Christian country over Easter, so he wasn't entitled to claim. You ever bloody heard anything like that?

Rosie Oh, dear.

Tommy I mean, I bet you an undercover Arab working over here—and there's plenty of 'em doing that—he'll be claiming for—whaddyacallit?— Ramadam, won't he? No, bloody '5, you forget them, darling.

Rosie Right.

Tommy You don't want to go joining them.

Rosie I won't.

A pause. Tommy jiggles around restlessly again

Tommy Fancy one, do you?

Rosie Sorry?

Tommy You fancy one? Before we get going? I mean, a lot of the girls do. I worked with some of them, they get, like, turned on just before the off. You know. You want to have a quick one just in case?

Rosie Just in case what?

Tommy Well, just in case. You know. That you don't make it, like. Not that
you're not going to make it. I'm here to see to that, don't you worry.

Rosie Glad to hear it.

Tommy What do you say, then? Fancy one, do you?

Rosie No, thank you.

Tommy Quick one? Only take five minutes?

Rosie No, not at all.

Tommy (*unoffended*) Suit yourself. Just that some girls do. Some of the girls,
they go barmy for——

Rosie Listen, do you think I could just have a moment's quiet, please? To
myself?

Tommy Why's that?

Rosie I need to—get into character.

Tommy (*mystified by this*) What's that, then?

Rosie If I'm to do this job properly, you see, I need a moment to concentrate
on being Joanna Rupelford. That's all.

Tommy Oh, right. Never heard of that before. Most of the girls, they
just——

Rosie Yes, well, I'm an exception.

Tommy Right. Suit yourself, then.

*Silence. Tommy starts his exercises again, shadow-punching and chopping
with the occasional kick-box. All accompanied by a series of grunts and
yelps. Rosie becomes increasingly irritated by this. She starts to retaliate with
a series of acting vocal warm-ups of her own, including scales and tongue-
twisters. As she grows louder, Tommy stops and stares at her in amazement.
He restarts his own warm-up with renewed vigour. The whole thing develops
into a sort of competition. However, when Tommy has grunted his last, Rosie
still manages a last glorious high note. She is undoubtedly the winner. Silence*

I used to have a girlfriend made noises like that. We could only ever have
it in the open air.

Rosie Good. Lucky her.

Pause

Tommy (*consulting his watch*) She's late, isn't she?

Rosie (*not being drawn*) Uh-huh.

Tommy I can go down to a depth of one mile wearing this watch.

Rosie I wish you would.

Tommy Useful. (*He now produces a short cosh-like implement from his belt.
He thwacks it against his palm a few times*) Know what this is, then?

Rosie Haven't the foggiest.

Tommy It's known as a CQT. Close-quarters truncheon. Cutie for short.
Special issue. (*He hits his palm again*) This could bring you to your knees,
like that. Put you out for a month. Want to feel it? Go on. Have a feel of that.
Rosie I don't want to feel it, thank you.
Tommy Really. Some girls, they love to——
Rosie Will you please shut up!
Tommy Right. Suit yourself.

A silence. Tommy brandishes the truncheon a few more times

I'll tell you one more thing, though——
Rosie (*thoroughly exasperated*) Oh, dear God!
Tommy No, no. Just one other thing. Even if you had this in your hand, even
armed with this, you would never get within a yard of me. Do you know
why that is?
Rosie No, I can't imagine.
Tommy Reflexes. I have incredible reflexes. They filmed me with the fastest
film they had and they still couldn't catch the speed of my hands. True.
When I was down there in Hereford, the instructor there told me I was
seriously frightening.
Rosie I know how he felt.
Tommy Come on, you have a try. Come on. Have a try.
Rosie No.
Tommy Come on.
Rosie No!
Tommy Come on, it'll make you feel better. You see how fast I move, it'll
make you feel better. Take it, go on, take it. (*He thrusts the cosh into Rosie's
reluctant hand*)
Rosie Oh, God.
Tommy That's it, that's it! Now you come at me. Tell you what, I'll be
behind the bar here, an innocent barman, you know. And you're coming
in to rob me. Pretend you're trying to rob me. Come on then, girl. Now you
come at me with the cosh, come and try hit me with it. And what I'll do,
you see, is block it with one hand and at the same time disarm you with the
other one. Now don't get nervous, I won't hurt you. Just try and hit me. Hit
me with it, hard as you like. And you'll be amaze——

Rosie hits Tommy on the head. He is unprepared

Rosie (*instantly appalled at what she's done*) Oh, God! I'm so sorry, I didn't
mean to...

Tommy sways and his knees buckle

Tommy (*feebly*) No, no. You got to wait till I'm ready, you see. Wait till I'm... (*He collapses behind the bar*)
Rosie (*alarmed*) Oh, no. (*She goes behind the bar*) Tommy! Tommy! (*She tries vainly to revive him*) Somebody. If you're listening. Help! Help me, please. I need help, whoever's listening. Sam! If you're——

The doorbell rings

Oh, thank God! (*She scurries to the front door and opens it*)

Edna is standing there holding a briefcase

Look, I've just done something—Oh, hallo, there.
Edna Miss Rupelford?
Rosie Yes?
Edna I called earlier.
Rosie Yes.
Edna But it wasn't convenient.
Rosie No.
Edna So. Here I am again.
Rosie Yes.

They stand there for a moment

Edna May I come in, dear?
Rosie Yes. (*She still doesn't move*)
Edna (*making to step forward*) Well?
Rosie (*stepping aside at last*) Yes. Sorry.

Edna steps into the flat and looks around her. Fortunately Tommy's inert body is hidden from view. Rosie reluctantly closes the front door

Edna Now obviously, I don't usually make house calls at this time of night but I'm happy to make this exception in your case, dear, since you're a new client. I would like to make this fairly quick if we could. I don't foresee any problems. I think we can find something to suit you. Isn't this a lovely flat? Aren't you lucky? And of course with the river there, you're not really overlooked at all, are you? I do envy you, dear. (*She places her briefcase on the table and opens it*)

It appears to be filled with make-up samples. Rosie stares at it

Now, if I can plunge straight in. From our brief acquaintance, you do have the most beautiful skin, dear, if I may say so... So you won't need a very heavy foundation. If I may be a wee bit critical, I think the one you're wearing at the moment is the tiniest bit heavy. I think we can go for something a shade lighter. Slightly creamier.

During the following Edna places Rosie on one of the bar stools and fastens a cape round her shoulders. This has the effect of pinioning Rosie's arms to her sides

What are we to make of this weather, then? The heat today! Almost suffocating, wasn't it? You could feel it, virtually sucking the breath out of you, couldn't you? Still, it's got to break sometime, that's what I say. Nothing lasts for ever, does it, dear? Not even beauty, alas. Now. (*She opens a jar*) I mean, I don't know how you feel about this as a shade for evening. It's just a whisper really, very subtle, just to give the skin the slightest hint of a glow. Here. (*She rubs some on the back of her hand*) What's your feeling on that, dear? Would you wear that?

Rosie (*thoroughly confused*) I'm sorry. I don't...

Edna Or maybe something in between, perhaps? (*She opens another jar and demonstrates again*) How about this? Now, this is our brand new range. We call it Entrapment. Isn't it beautiful? Again, just that hint of a sheen. We've only just launched it. I think that's even more you, dear, don't you? Yes, I do, it's you. It's definitely you.

Rosie Listen, I——

Edna Shall we settle for that for a minute, shall we? Now. Lipstick. (*She studies her*) Yes, I have to say I think you've gone for a shade too pale, dear. You've got such pretty lips, lovely mouth, you need to show it off, don't you? (*She selects a lipstick*) Now. This is very, very attractive. Quite popular with my ladies. It's called Promise of Dawn. May I, dear?

Rosie I really don't——

Before she can protest Edna has gently but firmly taken her chin and during the following carefully paints Rosie's mouth with a rather bright lipstick

Edna Beautiful. Oh, this is so you. This is so you, dear. It could have been made for you. I adore this shade, I love it to death, I really do. There. (*She admires her handiwork*) Yes. (*She holds up a small mirror*) What do you think? Isn't that you?

Rosie Listen, I don't know what's going on. I rather thought we were going to——

Edna Such a pretty mouth, haven't you?

Rosie (*starting to panic a bit*) I understood we were——

Edna Wait, wait, wait, dear. Don't be impatient. Must pretty you up first.

Now. What else can I interest you in? How about this, then? One second. (*She lifts the top panel out of the briefcase. Beneath are tightly packed packets of white powder*) Why don't you test a little of this?

Rosie looks at her

(*Pleasantly*) Take your time, dear. Make quite sure. I'm afraid we don't do refunds. (*She moves to the window and gazes out. Her eyes are never very far from Rosie, though*)

During the following, Rosie, rather self-consciously, starts to go through the testing ritual the way she has obviously been instructed to do. She lifts out a top packet and takes out one from underneath it. She opens it and tastes a sample on her finger

No, I just love your view. Always something going on, isn't there? Day or night. Is that Deptford across the river there?
Rosie Er, yes.
Edna No, I'm wrong, it's Rotherhithe. Surely it's Rotherhithe?
Rosie Yes. Rotherhithe.
Edna You finding that to your taste?
Rosie This is—is fine. Very good. First class.
Edna Good. Well, that was easy, wasn't it? One satisfied customer. (*She returns to Rosie*) I'll just hold on to my top tray of samples, if I may. You keep the case.
Rosie Thank you. (*She closes Edna's case and stands it on the floor*)
Edna Now, dear. The painful bit, I'm afraid.
Rosie What?
Edna Payment. The sordid part.
Rosie Oh, yes.
Edna I believe the price is agreed.
Rosie Oh, yes. Would you mind? (*She indicates for Edna to move the cosmetic tray off the coffee table*)
Edna Yes, of course. (*She does so*)

Rosie runs her fingers under the rim of the coffee table

Rosie (*aware of Edna's gaze, nervously*) Just a second. (*She tries again*)
Edna It is hot, isn't it?
Rosie Sorry?
Edna I notice you're perspiring a little, dear.
Rosie Oh, yes.
Edna I have something for that as well, if you'd like to try it?

Rosie No, no. I'll be fine.

The coffee table clicks open

There!
Edna Oh, how ingenious.
Rosie Here we are. (*She takes out the briefcase concealed in the hidden compartment*) Sorry about that. (*She is about to put Edna's briefcase away instead*)
Edna Oh, no, no, no.

Rosie freezes

Have to count it first, dear.
Rosie Sorry.

Edna places the second briefcase on the coffee table, forcing the compartment to close. She opens the case. It is filled with newspaper. Edna lifts the newspaper to examine deeper into the case. It contains yet more newspaper

Edna (*her voice hardening for the first time*) What's this?
Rosie What?
Edna Is this a joke?
Rosie What?
Edna (*tipping the contents on the floor*) This.
Rosie (*horrified*) But it was—it was—how did that happen? It was full of money. I've just this minute checked it. It was full of money. I swear it was.
Edna (*flicking some of the newspaper at Rosie*) Little short of a miracle, then. So where's the money? Where's my money, dear?
Rosie (*retreating*) I——
Edna (*advancing*) I'll ask you again nicely, dear. Where—is—my—money?
Rosie I don't know.
Edna Well, that rather rules out an exchange of goods then, doesn't it?
Rosie I'm sorry. I can't think what could have——
Edna But the problem is, you see, dear, that the people I work for are not going to be at all happy about this. Because every time I make this sort of journey, it costs me time and them money. And being very careful people they don't like to see either of those wasted.
Rosie Well, could you just tell them, please, that I'm very, very sorry indeed.
Edna Not to mention the risk involved in my coming here. Still, I'm sure they'll understand. And I know they'd like me to give you a free sample so you'll remember in the future, dear, never to waste my time again. (*She*

takes a spray bottle from her tray. She removes the cap) Just a little one. Come on. *(She points it at Rosie's face)*

Rosie jumps up and retreats in alarm

Come on, dear. Just a little squirt. I'll make it quick. Come here.

Rosie reaches the desk and ducks behind it

Rosie *(to the desk)* Help! Somebody come and help me.

Edna sprays some of the liquid on the desk. Rosie springs away as it narrowly misses her

Edna Oh, I am sorry, dear, that's going to ruin the surface of your lovely desk.
Rosie *(vainly)* Help!
Edna 'Fraid nobody can hear you, dear.

Rosie backs into the dining area

Rosie Some pussy cat. *(To the dining table)* Help me, please, help me!
Edna Come here, dear, don't keep running away. *(She sprays some more liquid)* You're not going to have any furniture left at this rate, are you?
Rosie HELP ME!!

Rosie rushes off to the bedroom

Edna makes to follow, then stops. Instead, she switches off the lights, conceals herself and waits. She hums softly to herself

In time, Rosie creeps back cautiously

Edna springs out and fires the spray again. Rosie wards this off with a kitchen chair. She makes for the front door again, but Edna is too close behind her

(Passing Tommy's still inert body) Wake up, you idiot!

The two women do another lap around the kitchen. Rosie darts into the living-room once more, where Edna catches her and forces Rosie across the armchair

Edna *(poised)* That's it. Close your eyes. It will only sting for a second. It's not going to kill you, dear. Just a little reminder...

Rosie This has been the worst day of my life... (*She closes her eyes*)

Edna prepares to spray her

Suddenly the door flies open and Tracy comes in like a whirlwind

Edna half-turns but is too late. She collapses under a hail of jabs and blows from Tracy. The spray flies out of her hand. Tracy stands over her, triumphant in her moment of glory

Maurice and Sam arrive in the doorway behind her

Maurice Beautifully done, Tracy. Very good indeed.

Sam dashes forward to Rosie

Sam Rosie? Are you all right? Rosie?
Rosie (*stunned with shock*) Huuuhhh!
Sam (*alarmed*) Rosie!
Rosie Huuuhhh! Huuuhhh!
Maurice She'll be all right. She's just in mild shock.
Rosie Miillddd?

Tracy has retrieved Edna's spray and is sniffing it cautiously

Maurice What is that stuff, Tracy, any idea?
Tracy Seems to be basically mildly diluted H_2SO_4.
Maurice Sulphuric acid.
Tracy Right.
Maurice That'll do it. That'd clear up your blackheads, wouldn't it?
Sam (*still with Rosie*) Deep breaths. Just take deep breaths.

Rosie slowly starts to recover

Maurice Where the hell is that oaf Tommy? Tommy!

From behind the bar, Tommy wakes up. He attempts to spring to his feet, ever the man of action, but his head is evidently very painful

Tommy Hah!
Maurice Congratulations, Tommy. Another successful mission. Girl's half-dead and someone's waltzed off with all the money. A highly satisfactory night's work. Well done!

Tommy (*still half-dazed*) Thank you very much, sir!

Maurice (*yelling*) YOU INCOMPETENT IDIOT!

Tommy Sir!

Maurice Now give Tracy a hand. Get this woman out of here. God, you haven't killed her, have you, Tracy?

Tracy I may have broken a few things, sir.

Maurice Oh, that's all right. So long as she's still alive. We might still get something out of her. Take her away, then.

Tracy and Tommy half-drag Edna's inert body through the front door

(*To Sam*) How's our little heroine?

Sam She's—I think she'll be OK.

Rosie (*still recovering*) Sam.

Sam I'm here, Rosie.

Rosie Oh, Sam. (*She clings to him*)

Maurice (*drily*) She'll be all right. More to the point, where's all the money gone? Rosie? Do you know?

Rosie What?

Maurice Where's the money?

Rosie I don't know, do I?

Maurice Haven't taken it, have you?

Rosie (*indignantly*) Why should I take it?

Maurice All right, all right!

Rosie Do you think I'd take it and risk my own life? Do you think I'm that stupid?

Maurice Yes, all right, all right. Just exploring every avenue. Well, there's going to be one hell of an inquest, that's all I can say. There was the best part of three quarters of a million quid in there. (*He begins to pick up the briefcase*) Well, at least we've got the drugs. I mean it was always going to be a risk, setting Edna loose with the money. But I think that was termed a justifiable risk. I don't know what you'd call it now. A pig's ear, I think. Nonetheless, Miss Seymore, you were superb. The next time you are appearing anywhere, I shall he there applauding and throwing roses. I can only apologize, on this occasion, for the distinct ropiness of some of your supporting cast. You're going to see her safely home, Sam?

Sam I'll see her home.

Maurice I think we might run to a taxi on this occasion. I'll switch all the gear off next door, Sam, don't you worry about it. In case you both wish to effect a tender reunion unrecorded and off-camera. Then I'm straight home to my bed.

Sam Thank you, sir.

Maurice Goodnight, Rosie. I'll forward on your expenses. If I'm not in jail. 'Bye.

Rosie 'Bye.
Sam 'Night, sir.
Maurice (*going*) God, what a cock-up.

Maurice goes out with the two briefcases and closes the front door behind him

Rosie I was calling. I was yelling my head off, what happened?
Sam We—we didn't know about Tommy, you see.
Rosie You didn't see what happened?
Sam No, at that point, of course, Edna hadn't arrived in the building and we—weren't actually on full alert. Technically.
Rosie What were you on?
Sam I mean, the monitor screens were on, of course, but—we were—we were, well, the technician had turned down the mics and switched over to the baseball so we weren't——
Rosie (*incredulously*) Baseball?
Sam The Cubs and the Padres.
Rosie You were all watching baseball?
Sam Very, very briefly. As soon as Edna arrived we were on you. All the time.
Rosie While she was chasing me round the room with an acid spray? I hope you caught that bit, did you?
Sam Well, we thought Tommy was—and then when he didn't intervene, of course, we decided to send in Tracy. I mean, you can't have too many people or they all get in each other's way. You can't have too many.
Rosie I'd have settled for one. Preferably you.
Sam I'm sorry.

Pause

I let you down again, didn't I?

Pause

Do you want me to phone you a taxi? I mean, I needn't come with you, if you'd rather…

Pause

Would you prefer me to leave now? I'll leave now, if you'd rather.
Rosie No, I don't want you to leave now. This has been the worst day of my life and I refuse to end it like this. I want us to go to bed now. Together.

Sam Are you sure?

Rosie I started today wanting more than anything else to forget everything and get laid. And I'm bloody well going to get laid, if it's the last thing I do. And if I die in the night, and on current form I could well do, then at least I might die with a smile on my face. (*She stares at Sam*) At least I hope I will.

Sam I'll do my best.

Rosie (*moving to the bedroom door*) I expect a lot more than that. I'm going to have a quick shower. Be there.

Sam (*smiling*) Yes, ma'am.

Rosie goes

Sam stands for a moment. He looks up briefly at the cameras. He moves swiftly to the front door. Looks out briefly. Closes it and goes to the coffee table, where he opens the secret compartment. He slides back a concealed flap and extricates the original briefcase. He closes the table again, opens the briefcase and examines the contents. The money is all there, intact

(*Softly*) Hidden depths. Now you see it, now you don't.

Rosie (*off; calling*) Sam!

Sam darts round the back of the bar. He crouches down and tucks the briefcase out of sight

Rosie comes in from the bedroom. She has a towel round her

Sam, I am absolutely starving, is there a—? (*She goes into the kitchen, puzzled. Alarmed*) Sam? (*In panic, a mighty yell*) SAM!!

Sam pops up from behind the bar rather guiltily

Sam Hi!

Rosie Sam...

Sam You all right?

Rosie I thought you'd gone again.

Sam No, I was—tidying up.

Rosie (*puzzled*) You were?

Sam Just—briefly.

Rosie Well, please come to bed now. I don't want you out of my sight again.

Sam OK. Can I just—?

Rosie No. You cannot just do anything. You are coming to bed. This instant.

Sam Fine. I just wanted to say...

Rosie What?
Sam Tomorrow.
Rosie What about it?
Sam I would like to take you away.
Rosie You would?
Sam To the very best hotel I can find.
Rosie Really? Where?
Sam Italy. Possibly. Then on from there, who knows?
Rosie Italy? To the best hotel? Can we afford that?
Sam I've just been given a bonus.
Rosie Well. I've never been taken to Italy. Not on a date. Actually, I've
    seldom made it further than the bed-and-breakfast on the corner. Italy.
    Great. We could have our gnocchi at long last, couldn't we?
Sam (*kissing her*) Plenty of gnocchi... Much, much gnocchi...
Rosie (*surfacing, at last*) Oh, Sam! Tomorrow's going to be better, isn't it?
    Tell me it is. Promise me tomorrow's going to be better...
Sam I solemnly promise you, Rosie, that tomorrow is going to be the most
    wonderful day of your life.
Rosie (*romantically*) Oh, Sam, I nearly believe you.

They go off happily to the bedroom, clinging to each other

A pause

The front door opens and Tracy enters. She carries a light hold-all

*She pauses, listening intently. She gazes up at the hidden cameras. We hear,
in the distance, the shower running and a squawk from Rosie as she
apparently steps under the initially freezing water. Tracy goes behind the
bar. She takes out the briefcase and places it on the counter. Swiftly she
transfers the money to the hold-all, zips it up and, closing the now empty
briefcase, replaces that behind the bar*

*Unseen by her, Maurice silently enters through the front door behind her.
He too listens for a moment*

A yell from Sam

Maurice Silly, silly boy...

*Tracy turns to look at him. She smiles. For the first time a genuinely warm
smile. She swings the hold-all. Maurice smiles at her. Tracy moves to him,
unhurriedly. Maurice waits. She hands him the hold-all. He hugs her. She*

*responds. He kisses her gently on the forehead. She kisses him gently in
response. We will never be able to guess at the nature of their relationship,
but we can gather it is deeply felt and mutual. A squeal of pleasure from Rosie
in the shower. Maurice and Tracy both look back towards the bedroom
doorway again*

(*Shaking his head, sadly*) Best of luck, Rosie. You'll need it, old thing.

Maurice places an arm around Tracy and they both go out of the front door

*As they go, more sounds of merriment from the shower. As the front door
closes behind them, the Lights fade rapidly to Black-out*

CURTAIN

FURNITURE AND PROPERTY LIST

Further dressing may be added at the director's discretion

ACT I

SCENE 1

On stage: Well-stocked bar
Glasses
Bar stools
Desk. *On it*: book
Chair
Sofa
Armchair
Heavy coffee table with hidden compartment
Pot plants
Hi-fi
CD rack containing 2 CDs
Small dining table
Four chairs
Domestic watering can
Sink with taps (practical) in kitchen
Kitchen roll
Kettle
Rosie's bag containing mobile phone

Personal: **Annette**: large set of master keys
Rosie: notebook, pencil

SCENE 2

Set: Make-up case in **Rosie**'s bag
Bottle of red wine in carrier bag
Corkscrew
Chopping board
Saucepan

Assorted cutlery in drawer
Apron in drawer

Off stage: Cartons and carrier bags containing gnocchi verde mixture and
            flour (**Sam**)

Personal: **Sam**: mobile phone
          Maurice: walkie-talkie, handkerchief, mobile phone
          Rosie: handcuffs
          Tracy: key

ACT II

SCENE 1

Set: Keys in **Rosie's** bag

Off stage: Key (**Maurice**)

SCENE 2

Set: Briefcase filled with newspaper

Off stage: Briefcase full of high-denomination notes (**Tommy**)
          Briefcase containing make-up samples, lipstick, spray bottle, cape,
            panel, packets of white powder (**Edna**)
          Light hold-all (**Tracy**)

Personal: **Tommy**: wrist-watch, short cosh

LIGHTING PLOT

Property fittings required: nil
1 interior. The same throughout

ACT I, SCENE 1

To open: Bright sunshine

Cue 1   **Rosie**: "What the hell are you doing, girl?"   (Page 13)
Fade to black-out

ACT I, SCENE 2

To open: Daylight outside fading. Practicals on

Cue 2   **Rosie** switches off a light or so   (Page 15)
Snap off practicals in sequence

Cue 3   **Rosie**: "What a day!"   (Page 38)
Fade to black-out

ACT II, SCENE 1

To open: Evening lighting

Cue 4   **Maurice**: "It's showtime."   (Page 47)
Fade to black-out

ACT II, SCENE 2

To open: Evening lighting

Cue 5   **Edna** switches off the lights   (Page 58)
Snap off practicals and covering spots

Cue 6   **Maurice** and **Tracy** exit   (Page 64)
Fade rapidly to black-out

EFFECTS PLOT

ACT I

Cue 13   **Rosie** answers phone   (Page 18)
              Cut phone ringing

Cue 14   **Rosie** switches off music   (Page 18)
              Party boat passing with thumping disco beat

Cue 15   **Rosie** puts on other CD   (Page 18)
              After a moment play "Paddy McGinty's Goat"

Cue 16   **Rosie** turns off music   (Page 19)
              Cut music

Cue 17   **Sam**: "Right, isn't it wonderful?"   (Page 24)
              Phone on desk ringing loudly, continuing

Cue 18   **Rosie** answers phone   (Page 25)
              Cut phone ringing

Cue 19   **Rosie**: "I don't believe this."   (Page 27)
              Pleasure boat passing outside

Cue 20   **Rosie** cries for a while   (Page 27)
              Doorbell rings briefly, and again after a moment

Cue 21   **Maurice**: "9-4. Check."   (Page 29)
              Walkie-Talkie as page 29

Cue 22   **Maurice**: "Welcome fair to moderate. Check." (Page 29)
              Walkie-Talkie as page 29

Cue 23   **Maurice** moves to window   (Page 29)
              Muffled sound of pleasure boat passing

ACT I

Cue 24   **Maurice**: "…and bury her mother."   (Page 46)
              After a pause, phone rings, continuing

Cue 25   **Rosie** answers phone   (Page 46)
              Cut phone ringing

Cue 26   **Tracy**: "…testing—1-2-3-4-5…"   (Page 47)
              Walkie-Talkie as page 47

Effects Plot

Cue 27	**Tracy**: "Desk … testing—1-2-3-4-5…" *Walkie-Talkie as page 47*	(Page 47)
Cue 28	**Tracy**: "Dining table … testing—1-2-3-4-5…" *Walkie-Talkie as page 47*	(Page 47)
Cue 29	**Tracy**: "Kitchen … testing—1-2-3-4-5…" *Walkie-Talkie as page 47*	(Page 47)
Cue 30	**Tracy**: "All working?" *Walkie-Talkie as page 48*	(Page 48)
Cue 31	**Tracy**: "That's the lot, then." *Walkie-Talkie as page 48*	(Page 48)
Cue 32	**Rosie**: "Sam! If you're——" *Doorbell rings*	(Page 54)
Cue 33	**Tracy** gazes up at hidden cameras *Distant sound of shower running*	(Page 63)

Lightning Source UK Ltd.
Milton Keynes UK
UKOW05f1924301116
288948UK00016B/571/P